POWER, NEOLIBERALISM, AND
THE REINVENTION OF POLITICS

PENN STATE SERIES IN CRITICAL THEORY

Eduardo Mendieta, General Editor

The Penn State Series in Critical Theory showcases the work of contemporary critical theorists who are building upon and expanding the canon of the Frankfurt School. Based on a series of symposia held at Penn State University, each volume in the series contains an original essay by an internationally renowned critical theorist, followed by a set of critical essays from a number of authors as well as the theorist's response to these essays. Books in the series will focus especially on topics that have been previously neglected by the Frankfurt tradition, including colonialism and imperialism, racism, sexism, and ethnocentrism. They offer analyses and readings that show the continuing relevance of one of the most innovative intellectual traditions of the last century.

Other books in the series:

Amy Allen and Eduardo Mendieta, eds., *From Alienation to Forms of Life: The Critical Theory of Rahel Jaeggi*

Amy Allen and Eduardo Mendieta, eds., *Justification and Emancipation: The Critical Theory of Rainer Forst*

Amy Allen and Eduardo Mendieta, eds., *Decolonizing Ethics: The Critical Theory of Enrique Dussel*

Power, Neoliberalism, and the Reinvention of Politics

The Critical Theory of Wendy Brown

EDITED BY AMY ALLEN AND EDUARDO MENDIETA

The Pennsylvania State University Press
University Park, Pennsylvania

Library of Congress Cataloging-in-Publication Data

Names: Allen, Amy, 1970– editor. | Mendieta,
    Eduardo, editor.
Title: Power, neoliberalism, and the reinvention of
    politics : the critical theory of Wendy Brown /
    edited by Amy Allen and Eduardo Mendieta.
Other titles: Penn State series in critical theory.
Description: University Park, Pennsylvania : The
    Pennsylvania State University Press, [2022] | Series:
    Penn State series in critical theory | Includes
    bibliographical references and index.
Summary: "A collection of essays introducing and
    assessing the work of political theorist Wendy
    Brown. Includes an original essay by Brown and a
    reply to her critics"—Provided by publisher.
Identifiers: LCCN 2022019081 | ISBN 9780271093345
    (paperback)
Subjects: LCSH: Brown, Wendy, 1955– | Political
    science—Philosophy. | Neoliberalism. | Power
    (Social sciences) | Critical theory. | Feminist
    theory. | LCGFT: Essays.
Classification: LCC JA71 .P719 2022 | DDC 320.01—
    dc23/eng/20220623
LC record available at https://lccn.loc.gov/2022019081

The Pennsylvania State University Press is a member
of the Association of University Presses.

It is the policy of The Pennsylvania State University
Press to use acid-free paper. Publications on uncoated
stock satisfy the minimum requirements of American
National Standard for Information Sciences—
Permanence of Paper for Printed Library Material,
ANSI Z39.48-1992.

CONTENTS

vi

ACKNOWLEDGMENTS

First and foremost, we want to express our deepest gratitude to Wendy Brown, who agreed to be subject of the symposium held April 19–20, 2019, at Penn State, on which this volume is based. Wendy cheerfully submitted her ideas to the critical scrutiny of many colleagues who have been studying her work for decades and patiently waited for finalized drafts of the chapters included here, notwithstanding her own very busy schedule. Then, in her concluding chapter, she engaged both critically and creatively with the different themes, topics, and questions raised by her interlocutors. She is not only a political philosopher of the first rank, a thinker who has contributed to feminist political philosophy and democratic theory in indispensable and pioneering ways, but also a warm and generous interlocutor and colleague. We also want to thank the contributors to this volume for their brilliant work and for their patience with the editing process, which was delayed by all sorts of unforeseen events, not least of all the Covid-19 pandemic. We are deeply thankful to them for their outstanding contributions. A special thank-you to Asad Haider for agreeing to expand his short comments at the symposium into a full paper. Thanks also to Martin Hartmann and Rahel Jaeggi for their insightful and engaging participation in the symposium, and to Penn State graduate students Wayne Wapeemukwa, Mercer Gary, and Jerome Clarke for chairing sessions and introducing speakers.

We are grateful to the departments of philosophy, political science, and women's, gender, and sexuality studies at Penn State for their generous financial, intellectual, and logistical support of the symposium on which this book is based. Eduardo would like to express his gratitude to Matthias Lutz-Bachmann and Thomas Schmidt for their invitation to be a research fellow at the Forschungskolleg Humanwissenschaften of the Goethe University in Bad Homburg, Germany, where his contribution to this volume was finalized. Heartfelt thanks also to Rachael Murphy, who coordinated all the details of the symposium, from travel, hotels, and visas to meals, publicity, and program design. It was a delight to work with her. Finally, we express our deepest gratitude to the team at

Penn State University Press: Kendra Boileau, our editor, for her enthusiasm, support, and patience; and Josie DiNovo and Ryan Peterson, for their diligence, efficiency, and professionalism. We are excited to see our productive partnership with the press grow and expand into an important and timely series.

Amy Allen and Eduardo Mendieta
STATE COLLEGE, PA

CHAPTER 1

Introduction

Amy Allen and Eduardo Mendieta

1. BROWN'S CRITICAL THEORY

In a 2017 interview, Wendy Brown offers the following definition of critical theory: "Critical theory for me, properly understood, involves an effort at apprehending this world. Such efforts can come from a lot of different traditions and sources. I would not confine critical theory to one school or lineage. Critical theory needs to be understood as something that subjects to critique both the approaches and norms of mainstream disciplines and the powers and norms that organize our lives. By critique, I don't mean rejection, of course, but an attempt to critically understand the premises and the powers that are circulating in existing knowledge and human practices."[1] A few features of Brown's distinctive approach to critical theory stand out in this definition: first, her refreshing eclecticism, her willingness to think across and among different critical traditions, frameworks, and approaches; second, her critical negativism, which focuses first and foremost on analyzing relations of power, domination, oppression, derogation, and injustice, rather than on articulating a positive normative program that is tethered to some putatively ideal and purified theory; and finally, her practical and political orientation, which emphasizes the idea of critique as a *Zeitdiagnose*, a critical diagnosis of the actually existing world we live in.

These features are evident throughout Brown's impressive body of scholarly work, which draws on a variety of theoretical sources to develop a distinctive critique of late capitalist societies. Her early work is firmly rooted in the history of Western political theory from Aristotle through Machiavelli to Weber and Arendt, refracted through the lens of feminist theory. This early work aimed to show how gender, as what is predicated on the threat of violence and the demand for protection, was constitutive of the very field of the political and its study, political theory. As her work has developed, she has returned again and again to a few key theoretical touchstones: Marx, Weber, and Freud; the early Frankfurt School, especially Benjamin and Marcuse; the genealogies of Nietzsche and Foucault; and Derrida's political writings. Rather than dogmatically defending one theoretical paradigm against the others or getting mired in methodological and metatheoretical debates about whether these different strands of theory are compatible with one another, Brown simply puts them to work in the service of her own critical projects. In her hands, the productive interconnections between these different approaches are strikingly evident.

Brown's emphasis on the critique of power is evident from her first book, *Manhood and Politics*, a revised version of her dissertation published in 1988. Brown's study of the way that understandings of the political are entangled with masculinist ideas of virtue, honor, and glory throughout the Western political tradition concludes with a remarkable set of reflections on the concept of power. "Power," Brown observes, "is one of those things we cannot approach head-on or in isolation from other subjects if we are to speak about it intelligently."[2] Power is both "determining and elusive," "ubiquitous and also largely invisible."[3] Although her focus on power makes her highly attuned to relations of domination and subordination, her understanding of power is complex. Unlike feminists of the preceding generation, Brown resists the equation of power with domination and encourages feminists not to shy away from the exercise of power. Power may constrain and preserve, but it can also destabilize and generate. Adopting an understanding of power that is influenced by Arendt's notion of the capacity to act in concert and Foucault's emphasis on the productivity of power, Brown's feminism embraces both the risks and the possibilities that open up with the exercise of power. Power is the condition of possibility of both futurity and natality; it enables the opening of horizons of action that generate common futures. As she puts it, "[Feminists] need to get to know power as something other than an enemy, to recognize power as potency and not simply domination, as exciting and not only dangerous, as productive and not simply repressive or injurious."[4]

The concept of power moves closer to the forefront in Brown's second book, *States of Injury: Power and Freedom in Late Modernity*, published in 1995.[5] Here Brown further interrogates the complexities and ambivalences of contemporary power relations, with a particular focus on how theoretical and political projects that set out to resist domination all too often end up in unwitting complicity with it. A central concern of this text is to unravel how emancipatory aims are both watered down and subverted when political actors turn to the regulatory power of the state to redress existing relations of domination. The feminist critique of pornography, spearheaded by Catharine MacKinnon and the focus of so much feminist energy in the 1980s, serves as a crucial example of this phenomenon, though the phenomenon itself is not confined to feminist politics. If her 1988 book, *Manhood and Politics*, developed a genealogical critique of Western political philosophy by unmasking its constitutive masculinist foundations, in *States of Injury* Brown focuses on how the category of "gender" as deployed by anti-pornography feminists reinscribes gender as the site of violence and the attendant demand for statist protection. Interestingly, Brown allows us to recognize how gender becomes the means by which "the state of nature" gets reintroduced into civil society and the political as such.

The connections between relations of power and the formation of the desiring subject is also a core theme of this book. Indeed, her novel analysis of "wounded attachments"—those attachments to unfreedom and desires for domination, fueled by ressentiment, that afflict ostensibly emancipatory political movements such as feminism—stands out as one of the key conceptual contributions of this watershed text and facilitates a discerning critique of some of the problematic investments of late twentieth-century models of identity politics.

Brown's keen diagnosis of the limitations of existing critical paradigms continues in her 2001 book, *Politics Out of History*. In this text,

Brown paints a picture of critical theory at a crossroads, having thoroughly debunked modernist notions such as "progress, right, sovereignty, free will, moral truth, reason" but not yet having figured out what to put in their place.[6] Ever attentive to the seductions of reactionary forms of melancholia, Brown asks what new possibilities are opened up in this moment of destabilization: "how we might conceive and chart power in terms other than logic, develop historical political consciousness in terms other than progress, articulate our political investments without notions of teleology and naturalized desire, and affirm political judgment in terms that depart from moralism and conviction."[7] The breakup of modernist narratives of historical progress, notions of epistemological foundations, and sovereignty and rights discourses creates new anxieties but also opens up new possibilities. In a core chapter, Brown intervenes in debates between Marxists and poststructuralists by making explicit their disagreements about power. Tracing the logic of power in Marx's work, she explores the ways that Marx's critique of capitalist power relations is intertwined with the progressive, dialectical logic of history that undergirds his work and challenges critical theorists to rethink the grounds of critique in ways that "work free of these logics."[8] Later essays in this volume offer critical reappropriations of Nietzsche, Benjamin, Foucault, and Derrida that provide resources for rethinking politics in a way that is attentive to historical context without attributing a distinctive logic or trajectory to history.

Although her work has always been situated within its historical and political context, the emphasis on critique as an apprehension of the world has moved to the forefront of Brown's thinking in the last fifteen years. Whereas her earlier work was more oriented toward debates within feminist theory, the history of political thought, and contemporary political theory, her work undergoes a subtle yet discernible shift starting with *Regulating Aversion: Tolerance in the Age of Identity and Empire* (2006) away from textual debates and toward the development of an incisive critique of actually existing, late modern, neoliberal capitalist societies.[9] Her work continues to draw on a deep well of theoretical erudition—her critiques are grounded in sustained conversations with thinkers such as Freud, Foucault, Marcuse, Agamben, Hardt and Negri, Schmitt, Hayek, and others—but this erudition is now mobilized in the service of a diagnosis of our neoliberal and increasingly authoritarian times. One can see this shift in *Regulating Aversion* when she brings her argument about the depoliticizing and imperialistic effects of the liberal discourse of tolerance to bear on the politics of the Simon Wiesenthal Center's Museum of Tolerance, revealing how the museum's discourse of tolerance veils a demonization of Arabs as intolerant and therefore uncivilized—a move that fit well with the broader anti-Arab sentiment that was rampant in the United States in the early 2000s.

A similar shift of focus is evident in her 2010 book *Walled States, Waning Sovereignty*, which analyzes the paradoxical proliferation of walls marking national boundaries even as the sovereignty of nation-states is on the wane, in the process of being supplanted by the forces of global capitalism, inter- and transnational political institutions, and religion.[10] In a world in which the sovereignty of nation-states is in decline, walls and borders become telling symbols of national identification: hyperbolic, ostentatious displays of a sovereign might that is in eclipse. Brown's diagnosis of the psychic investment in walls as indicative of a desire for the restoration of national sovereignty on the part of subjects who have been made particularly vulnerable by its decline— for example, by the way that global capitalism has hollowed out the economies of the midwestern United States—is remarkably prescient. Although the book was published long before the 2016 presidential campaign began, Brown offers a compelling *ex ante* diagnosis of the crowds of Trump supporters chanting "Build the Wall!"

This practical-political turn comes to full expression in Brown's recent work on neoliberalism and authoritarianism. Her 2015 *Undoing the Demos: Neoliberalism's Stealth Revolution* draws on Foucault's work to develop an original analysis of what distinguishes neoliberalism from other forms or modalities of capitalism. For Brown this is less about economic policy and recalibrating the role of governments in welfare provision and more about the emergence of a specific form of political rationality in which every domain of human life comes to be understood in economic terms. The result is not only a fundamental reorientation of human social and political life but also a "conceptual unmooring and substantive disembowelment" of democracy "understood as rule by the people."[11] Thus, as Brown argues in her most recent book, *In the Ruins*

of Neoliberalism: The Rise of Antidemocratic Politics in the West, neoliberalism "prepared the ground for the mobilization and legitimacy of
ferocious antidemocratic forces in the second decade of the twenty-first
century."[12] Once again, Brown's analysis proves remarkably prescient:
her summary of the nihilism and ressentiment driving right-wing politics in the United States—"if white men cannot own democracy, there
will be no democracy"[13]—could serve as an equally compelling diagnosis of the attack on the US Capitol on January 6, 2021, which took place
two years *after* her book was published.

2. BROWN'S FEMINISM

Brown's approach to critical theory is distinctive not only for the three
features delineated above—her eclecticism, negativism, and practical-
political orientation—but also for its explicitly feminist character. Feminist concerns have animated Brown's work from the beginning, and
yet her relationship to academic feminism has also been a critical one.
Throughout her work, Brown has developed a compelling argument for
a fundamental reorientation of feminism away from a focus on the identity category of "women" and toward a broader focus on the intersectional dynamics of domination. The beginnings of this shift are already
evident in Brown's first book, *Manhood and Politics,* which "seeks to lay
bare, analyze critically, and ultimately press toward transformation" the
"relationship between manliness and politics, as it has been inscribed in
traditional political theory."[14] This focus, Brown insists, brings a feminist angle of vision to political theory but, unlike much of the work
in feminist political theory that preceded it, does so without dealing
"solely or even centrally with women."[15] Although it is undeniably true
that most political theorists in the Western canon of political theory
held misogynist views, Brown resists reducing feminism's contribution
to the criticism of these views. "That most political theorists of the past
refused women a place in the political order is beyond doubt, as is the
fact that this exclusion is not incidental nor easily rectified."[16] But to
focus feminist claims on how women have been denied political status
is to miss the opportunity to criticize the very conception of the politi-

cal from which they have been excluded. "The radical critical possibility of a feminist perspective on the tradition of political theory," for Brown, "lies in grasping the ways in which what we know as politics is a politics constructed according to specific notions, practices, and institutions of masculinity."[17] This is a shift away from women as an identity category toward discursive constructions of masculinity and their distorting and constraining effects. If women's demands for "inclusion," "representation," and "participation" in the political field necessitate accepting its very masculinist construction, then Brown urges us to reconfigure the field of the political as such, as well as what counts as political agency.

Still, Brown has also long been wary of the conclusions that many feminists have drawn from similar diagnoses of masculinism: that the solution is to re-center "feminine" values or modes of thought. Such an approach not only misses the point of analyzing masculinity and femininity as *discursive constructions*, which also means that they are developed under and shaped by conditions of domination and oppression, but is also difficult to sustain once we attend, as we must, to differences of race, class, culture, and religion.[18] Brown's vision of feminist politics instead counsels a move away from a politics that is predicated on the "domination of necessity and the body"[19] and toward the realization that the body is the "locus, vehicle, and origin of our freedom."[20] Although she doesn't note the connection, this view is highly resonant with the early Frankfurt School's critique of Enlightenment rationality as resting on the domination of inner nature and their recuperation of polymorphous perversity (Marcuse) and the ethical injunction to be a "good animal" (Adorno).[21]

Brown carries this critique of a feminist politics centered on women's identity further in her influential conceptualization of wounded attachments. Her essay of the same name investigates the problematic investments of contemporary identity-based politics. Given that gender and racial subordination are maintained and reproduced through identity categories, how, Brown asks, can the politicization of such categories avoid resubordinating the subject they aim to emancipate? Unpacking the seductive nature of identity, its unwitting reinforcement of the very universalistic liberal ideals from which it claims to be excluded, Brown identifies the tendency of politicized identity to become invested in its

7

own suffering and subordination, giving rise to a politics of ressentiment that inclines members of oppressed groups to "reproach power rather than aspire to it, to disdain freedom rather than practice it."[22] In order to break out of the self-reinforcing cycle by means of which identity can make political claims for itself only by further entrenching its own pain and suffering, Brown suggests a subtle yet decisive shift away from a politics based on identity ("I am") to one based on the articulation of the desire for a collective good ("I want for us").[23]

This argument comes to full expression in her groundbreaking and provocatively titled essay "The Impossibility of Women's Studies." Applying her analysis of the instability of identity categories to the intellectual rationale for the discipline of women's studies, Brown argues that this rationale has proved increasingly untenable. Without denying the tremendous historical importance of women's studies as a field, Brown contends that, as a contemporary academic discipline, women's studies is both theoretically incoherent and tacitly conservative: "incoherent because by definition it circumscribes uncircumscribable 'women' as an objective of study, and conservative because it must resist all objections to such circumscription if it is to sustain that object of study as its raison d'être."[24] If women's studies is to remain a site of radical scholarship and politics, and if it is to deploy the concept of gender critically and self-reflexively, then, Brown argues, the field must give up its focus on women and its concomitant conceptual subordination of race (and other axes of oppression) to gender. What is needed is a much broader set of conceptual tools—found in a wide range of disciplines, including history, psychoanalysis, political economy, legal theory, cultural studies, and political theory—that will enable us to analyze and produce fine-grained genealogies of crosscutting modes of subjection. Such a reorientation of the field, Brown admits, "will add up neither to a unified and coherent notion of gender nor to a firm foundation for women's studies. But it might allow us to take those powerful founding and sustaining impulses of women's studies . . . and harness them for another generation or two of productive, insurrectionary work."[25]

Situating Brown's feminism within the context of her relationship to critical theory, it is worth noting that she is one of a small handful of pioneering theorists—which includes such important figures as Seyla

Benhabib, Nancy Fraser, and Iris Marion Young—who staked out a distinctively feminist approach to critical theory starting in the late 1980s. However, Brown stands out among this very distinguished and influential group of theorists for her recuperation of the first generation of the Frankfurt School and her lack of interest in the Habermasian paradigm, even when that paradigm had been recast in light of feminist critique. As she notes in the introduction to her 2006 special issue of the journal *differences* on feminism and the Frankfurt School, "To the extent that feminist theory does engage this [Critical Theory] tradition today, it is primarily through Jürgen Habermas; and within Habermas's extensive oeuvre, it is his theorization of the public sphere and communicative rationality—his later, markedly Kantian and more liberal thinking—that feminist theory has taken up. And whatever the value of Habermas's work on communicative ethics, it cannot be said to bear the philosophical reach or political radicalism represented by the early Frankfurt School. So also, then, has something in feminist theory been tamed."[26] Like the early Frankfurt School thinkers whose philosophical reach and political radicalism Brown admires and emulates, her recent work infuses the critique of neoliberal capitalism with a psychoanalytic perspective, but unlike them, she keeps intersectional dynamics of subjection and oppression clearly in view. The result is an utterly original, highly productive, distinctively *feminist* critical theory.

3. NEOLIBERALISM: THE LATEST, HIGHEST, UGLIEST STAGE OF CAPITALISM

Like the first generation of critical theorists, as noted above, Brown has aimed to develop a critical theory that is attentive to subject formation, political psychology, and the political economy that establishes the modes of production and their concomitant social relations, without reducing any of these fields to the economic base. It may be said that what late capitalism was for Adorno, Horkheimer, Kirchheimer, Pollock, and Neumann, neoliberalism has been for Brown—namely, the prism through which to analyze new modes of exploitation and subordination but also of subject formation. As with the first generation, for whom the question of late capitalism was linked to the authoritarian personality and anti-Semitism, for Brown neoliberalism is linked to what she calls authoritarian freedom and an "aggrieved" and "wounded," unquestionably male, subjectivity. In her most recent books, *Walled States, Waning Sovereignty, Undoing the Demos*, and *In the Ruins of Neoliberalism*, Brown has developed one of the most sustained, extensive, detailed, and perspicacious analyses of this latest incarnation of late capitalism: neoliberalism.

It may be useful to foreground some key aspects of Brown's analysis of neoliberalism. First, for Brown neoliberalism means the eclipse, if not sequestration, of *homo politicus* by *homo oeconomicus*, in which politics has been reduced to serving the economy. All political issues are now subordinated to the self-interested and strategic pursuit of economic gain, uncoupled from political considerations or the common good. The eclipsing ascendancy of *homo oeconomicus* means the ideological and material dominance of a conception of the subject as a singularized, granularized, quantified, monadic economic unit. In neoliberalism, we are our work; literally, we alone are responsible for what we make of ourselves. We are our investments. And the economy is the guarantor of the field within which we all compete to make the best of our investment into the fund that we are.

Second, because neoliberalism singularizes the subject, detaching it from others, this subject can only experience social injury, derogation, and subordination, in terms of denied entitlements. The neoliberal subject, completely isolated, can only experience relationality in terms of aggrievement, resentment, comeuppance, and schadenfreude—namely, in forms of singularized affective states. The neoliberal subject, then, is the subject of the zero sum, for whom someone else's gain is its loss.

Third, this modality of individuated agency and subject formation that turns sociality into introjected affectivity (aggrieved woundedness) has given rise to what Brown calls authoritarian politics, a form of antidemocratic politics, that in fact is an antipolitical politics. This is arguably the most prescient and relevant feature of Brown's analysis of neoliberalism. Neoliberalism, which neutralizes politics by subordinating it to the economy, results in the potentiation of an antipolitical politics, a decisionist and authoritarian politics, a politics of "it's my way or the highway," an infantile, hysterical, visceral politics that does not accept the very terms of the political: deliberation, persuasion, compromise, and action in concert, all of which are oriented toward the common good and our collective future.

11

Fourth, and most innovatively, all of these analyses are brought together in Brown's fascinating analysis of freedom under neoliberal governmentality. Neoliberalism has unleashed a Frankenstein freedom, a freedom that turns authoritarian, antidemocratic, and antideliberation. As she puts it in the chapter that opens this book, "What Is Left of Freedom?": "We . . . need to ask what to do with freedom at a historical conjuncture when it has truly gone rogue, when it has been ripped from contexts through which it could support rather than destroy prospects of justice, eco-viability, and peaceful cohabitation, when the alchemy of neoliberalism, white male supremacy and nihilism has made freedom monstrous." Neoliberalism, which has weaponized an aggrieved, white, nihilistic, entitled, white masculinity—which we could now call embattled white freedom—has alchemized freedom into something violent, intolerant, unreasonable, and unsociable. This is no longer the freedom of either the ancients or the moderns but the freedom of the CEO, the Oath Keepers, the anti-maskers, and the white warriors of freedom for the few and exclusion for the many. Brown's most recent work constitutes a major contribution to the history of freedom in the age of the seeming exhaustion of collective movements of emancipation. Hers, then, is a genealogy of freedom with a practical and emancipatory intent.

4. OVERVIEW OF THE VOLUME

The chapters in this book provide us with an excellent overview of Brown's wide and rich scholarly corpus. Together they cover her contributions to feminist theory, the philosophy of history, political philosophy, the critical history of modern political philosophy, and the critical theory of neoliberalism. The volume opens with Brown's chapter "What Is Left of Freedom?," in which she takes up the question of how we should rethink the production of freedom in light of new projects of emancipation that aim to counter the corrosive effects of neoliberalism. As Brown argues, at no time has the invocation of freedom been so widespread and vociferous while simultaneously supporting such antidemocratic consequences. Brown forces the question: How is neoliberal freedom, or at least its version of economic freedom, a freedom that turns against liberation and emancipation for some while claiming absolute freedom for others? She argues that we have to conceive of emancipation projects that are guided by at least four key points. First, the freedom we affirm should not be conceived in terms of liberalism, which presupposes that freedom is an individual choice. This form of freedom is both unjust and irresponsible, as it is anti-ecological and antidemocratic. Second, the form of freedom we ought to seek is one that is tightly interwoven with responsibility—not as a limit of it but as its very core. Responsible freedom turns out to be a practice, an ethos, and not an afterthought. Third, responsible freedom is democratic freedom, a freedom that is lived out with others, for others, and aims to expand its ethos through education. Responsible and democratic freedom is the freedom of a democratic people, one that is educated into the democratic ethos of shared freedom. A democratic people, furthermore, does not invidiously juxtapose freedom and equality, where those on the right aim to subordinate equality to freedom, while those on the left argue on behalf of equality even if freedom is to be constrained. Brown argues for a dialectical, materialistic conception of both equality and freedom, or what Étienne Balibar has called "equaliberty."[27] From this perspective, freedom without equality is the privilege of some, while equality without freedom gives rise to a politics of aggrievement and resentment that turns antidemocratic in the name of putatively curtailed freedom. Finally, democratic freedom must ceaselessly and relentlessly confront all the different powers that are unleashed, and that appear indomitable, by our society. These powers are as much material as they are ideological, psychological, linguistic, or technological, and they permeate every facet of our collective life. We produce and achieve freedom under conditions and powers we ourselves generate. Thus, democratic freedom must continually demystify and unmask the alleged naturalness of the forms of subordination and oppression generated by powers we ourselves have produced.

Robyn Marasco's chapter follows the feminist thread that runs through Brown's published works and public lectures, from *Manhood and Politics* and the central debates of *States of Injury* to the later reflections on sovereignty in *Walled States, Waning Sovereignty*. Marasco argues for the importance of Brown's early theoretical formation to everything that came after and for the persistence of a feminist method across her works, despite an apparent shift away from feminist questions and concerns in her later writings. Feminism, in Marasco's analysis of Brown's work, is a theory of politics and practice of political critique. As such, Marasco's chapter demonstrates how Brown's version of feminism remains essential to critical theory and political science.

Loren Goldman's chapter offers a rejoinder to Brown's apparently pessimistic philosophy of history. Brown has criticized the notion of progress as leading to both apathy and enthusiasm: on the one hand, it allows resignation to history's inevitable development; on the other, it can excuse and even encourage present injustices in the service of an illusory, utopian future. Such concerns leave little room for hope that the world can become better, a sensibility that is crucial for Brown's own project and, indeed, any emancipatory political theory. The problem, Goldman argues, is that Brown views history monolithically despite herself: she leaves no space for what Ernst Bloch called its "nonsynchronicity," the fact that multiple historical tendencies exist simultaneously, with trajectories often at cross-purposes. Against Brown, he suggests that any given historical moment boasts nonsynchronous tensions that allow a political vision of a better future without entertaining a determinist progressive account of history. Most propitiously, Goldman's invocation of Bloch's generative concept of "synchronous nonsynchronicities" allows us to make sense of regressive and retrograde political movements such as Trumpism, with its appeals to take us back to a masculinist, misogynist, racist, militaristic, imperial "America" that would be "again great."

Eduardo Mendieta's chapter takes up issues discussed by Marasco and Goldman and brings them together through an analysis of Brown's project of a "genealogical politics." Mendieta considers the question of history and political agency, or how we make sense of political agency across history. After reconstructing Brown's account of genealogical politics, Mendieta turns to a close analysis of her genealogy of neo-liberal rationality and what she has called both "authoritarian freedom" and "neoliberal freedom." By focusing on this aspect of Brown's work, he foregrounds how neoliberalism has eroded and eviscerated demo-cratic politics. These issues fall under the sustained analysis of what Brown calls the "neoliberal revolution" and its pernicious effects on the political vernaculars of democratic politics in the United States. The chapter ends with a close look at what Brown calls the *femina domes-tica* of neoliberalism, a concept that reveals the "gendered and gender-ing" dimension of neoliberalism and the decidedly male character of *homo oeconomicus.*

Johanna Oksala's chapter extends this analysis of the role of gen-der in neoliberalism. The chapter uncovers two contrasting views of the political in Brown's thought—the political understood either as a distinct and substantive sphere in its own right or as the result of his-torically contingent struggles of politicization. Oksala argues that the tension between these two views produces some problematic conse-quences for Brown's analysis of neoliberalism. Her argument comprises two parts. In the first section, Oksala focuses mainly on Brown's cri-tique of neoliberalism in *Undoing the Demos.* There she poses questions to Brown regarding the figure of *homo politicus* central to the latter's argument. She also questions the distinction between the economic and political spheres underlying her critique. In the second section, Oksala shows how the tension between the two different conceptions of the political is connected to the strains in Brown's analyses of the contem-porary gendering of the political realm. She concludes by defending the importance of Marxist-feminist analyses of social reproduction for an adequate theoretical and political response to the current challenges that neoliberalism poses to feminist politics.

In "Four Concepts in Depoliticized Politics," Asad Haider provides us with a rich analytical lexicon of Brown's political philosophy and its usefulness. Haider approaches the problem of the closure of politics in the context of neoliberalism and authoritarian populism by emphasiz-ing four key terms in and relating to Brown's work: depoliticization, subject, reproduction, and repression. Each of these terms is explored, defined, and mobilized within Brown's texts and evaluated according to specific genealogies and conceptual lines of demarcation.

In his chapter, Robin Celikates builds on Brown's diagnosis of the neoliberal program of "undoing the demos" and the right-wing reaction to it, distinguishing between different forms of depoliticization and repoliticization that complicate contemporary discourses on authoritarianism and populism(s). While on the surface both left-wing movements such as Occupy and more recent right-wing movements in Europe and the United States seem to respond to the neoliberal evacuation of the political by employing strategies of hyperpoliticization, Celikates argues that right-wing authoritarianism is better understood as mobilizing a dynamic of pseudopoliticization that is ultimately antipolitical. In Celikates's analysis, this form of antipolitical pseudopoliticization ends up contributing to the further "undoing of the demos" rather than to its "remaking." Returning to the scene of politicization "from the left," Celikates sketches out some implications for the debate about "left populism" and the problem of political form, before ending with some remarks on what a radical-democratic remaking of the demos—a remaking that also presupposes an undoing, albeit a different one—might look like.

In line with the format of our volumes in this series, the book closes with a chapter in which Brown responds to contributors to this volume, addressing the various criticisms and questions raised in their respective contributions. After responding to some of these provocations, Brown's chapter concludes our volume by sketching some of the worldly predicaments inviting political theoretical study and imagination today. These include the interregnum between nation-states and globalized powers, the neoliberal fragmentation of society and delegitimation of democracy, the emergence of disinformed and affectively charged electorates, widespread nihilism and fatalism, and political emergencies such as the climate and biodiversity crises. Against the backdrop of these predicaments, Brown also considers the multifold challenges to democracy as idea and practice, from critiques of humanism, to democracy's imbrication with colonialism, to climate change. The chapter, and our volume, concludes by challenging theorists to turn toward rather than away from these difficulties.

NOTES

1. "Interview—Wendy Brown," E-International Relations, April 25, 2017, available online at: https://www.e-ir.info/2017/04/25/interview/.

2. Wendy Brown, *Manhood and Politics: A Feminist Reading in Political Theory* (Totowa, NJ: Rowman & Littlefield, 1988), 207.

3. Ibid., 207.

4. Ibid., 209.

5. Wendy Brown, *States of Injury: Power and Freedom in Late Modernity* (Princeton: Princeton University Press, 1995).

6. Wendy Brown, *Politics Out of History* (Princeton: Princeton University Press, 2001), 4.

7. Ibid., 4.

8. Ibid., 90.

9. Wendy Brown, *Regulating Aversion: Tolerance in the Age of Identity and Empire* (Princeton: Princeton University Press, 2009).

10. Wendy Brown, *Walled States, Waning Sovereignty* (New York: Zone Books, 2010).

11. Wendy Brown, *Undoing the Demos: Neoliberalism's Stealth Revolution* (New York: Zone Books, 2015).

12. Wendy Brown, *In the Ruins of Neoliberalism: The Rise of Antidemocratic Politics in the West* (New York: Columbia University Press, 2019), 7.

13. Ibid., 180.

14. Brown, *Manhood and Politics*, 4.

15. Ibid., 10.

16. Ibid., 12.

17. Ibid.

18. See ibid., 189–91.

19. Ibid., 199.

20. Ibid., 196.

21. Theodor W. Adorno, *Negative Dialectics*, trans. E. B. Ashton (New York: Seabury Press, 1973), 299. See also Herbert Marcuse, *Eros and Civilization: A Philosophical Inquiry into Freud* (Boston: Beacon Press, 1966).

22. Brown, *States of Injury*, 55.

23. Ibid., 75.

24. Wendy Brown, *Edgework: Critical Essays on Knowledge and Politics* (Princeton: Princeton University Press, 2005), 120.

25. Ibid., 131.

26. Wendy Brown, "Feminist Theory and the Frankfurt School: Introduction," *differences: A Journal of Feminist Cultural Studies* 17, no. 1 (2006): 2.

27. See Étienne Balibar, *Equaliberty: Political Essays*, trans. James Ingram (Durham: Duke University Press, 2014).

CHAPTER 2

What Is Left of Freedom?

Wendy Brown

In his visit with [Kanye] West, the rapper T.I. was stunned to find that
West, despite his endorsement of Trump, had never heard of the travel
ban. "He don't know the things that we know because he's removed
himself from society to a point where it don't reach him," T.I. said.
West calls his struggle the right to be a "free thinker," and he is, indeed,
championing a kind of freedom—a white freedom, freedom without
consequence, freedom without criticism, freedom to be proud and
ignorant; freedom to profit off a people in one moment and abandon
them in the next; a Stand Your Ground freedom, freedom without
responsibility, without hard memory; a Monticello without slavery, a
Confederate freedom, the freedom of John C. Calhoun, not the freedom
of Harriet Tubman, which calls you to risk your own; not the freedom of
Nat Turner, which calls you to give even more, but a conqueror's freedom,
freedom of the strong built on antipathy or indifference to the weak, the
freedom of rape buttons, pussy grabbers, and *fuck you anyway, bitch*;
the freedom of oil and invisible wars, the freedom of suburbs drawn with
red lines, the white freedom of Calabasas.

—TA-NEHISI COATES, "I'M NOT BLACK, I'M KANYE"[1]

Democracy. . . . Isn't that where other people tell you what to do?

—INTERVIEWEE IN *WHAT IS DEMOCRACY?*, A FILM BY ASTRA TAYLOR

How have we arrived at what may be the most irresponsible, antisocial, and undemocratic understandings and practices of freedom in modern Western history? Practices that make child's play of the anarchy Plato warned against as democracy's fallen state. Of classic liberal anxieties about the unwashed masses wasting liberty for indulgence rather than self-improvement. Of neo-aristocratic worries about the masses having too much say and sway in republics. Today, freedom is the contrivance by which already broken political and social orders are further dismembered and degraded, by which social justice is attacked as totalitarian while authoritarian political power is legitimated, by which racial, gendered, and sexual hierarchies are resecured through conservative Christian annexations of heretofore secular provinces of public and economic life. It is the auspice for flouting public health ordinances, for refusing science and fact on disease and climate change, for waving Confederate flags, for assembling and speaking out as ethnonationalists and even ethnic cleansers, and for carrying guns into restaurants, bars, workplaces, and statehouses. At the same time, it is under these auspices that women are denied control of their reproductive lives, queers are barred from marriage, and Muslims are punished for modest dress. It is the rubric for reintroducing Christian prayer in schools and eliminating textbooks on evolutionary science. Above all, freedom has become a sharp instrument for attacking democracy itself. How did freedom get here?

This chapter begins by reflecting on the problematic of human freedom as emerging from the distinctly human project of political rule and the singularly human capacity to generate orders of power that slip our control. It then considers how freedom has been configured within the antidemocratic authoritarian liberalism taking shape in many parts of the globe today. If classical liberalism's identification of freedom as a private, individual good quietly ignored social powers of inequality, marginalization, and abjection that bear on its use, *antidemocratic authoritarian liberalism* is the political form converting liberty into a rabid defense of those powers. Divested from popular sovereignty in particular and democracy and democratization in general, and animated by the unprecedented social disintegration of neoliberalism, freedom within this form is more than anti-statist. It is antidemocratic, antipolitical, antisocial, and sometimes anti-life. As "they want to take your freedom away" provides cover for everything from corporate plunder to climate denialism, from commercial exclusions of LGBTQ patrons to exclusions of insurance coverage for contraception and abortion, from military-grade-weapons ownership to racist and misogynist social media screeds, this iteration of freedom has been sharpened as a potent weapon against a politics of equality, a politics of care, and a politics reckoning with ecological limits. Perhaps such sharpening is an unconscious protest against the incomparably complex and daunting powers of the age. Perhaps it is a protest against demands to care for others and the earth when caring for one's own is inordinately challenging. Perhaps its spirit—freedom against responsibility, society, democracy, inclusion, equality, life, and futurity—reflects the violent death spiral of modern white masculinist supremacy, a regime for which entitlement to exploit, subjugate, plunder, and kill has long been wrapped in freedom's mantle.[2] Routinized and institutionalized for centuries in practices of Native land dispossession, chattel slavery, lynching, racist policing, and patriarchal law and violence, today this entitlement has gone feral.

19

Still, if hegemonic forms and practices of freedom in the West have always been saturated with the right to dominate and exploit those excluded from it, then more than freedom's recent mobilization by the hard Right is responsible for our disorientation about political freedom today. There is also the steady surfacing—especially by feminists and anti-racists—of freedom's imbrication with stratification, domination, and violence. "We remain burdened by the question posed by eighteenth-century English poet and essayist Samuel Johnson," Jefferson Cowie writes. "'Why do we hear the loudest yelps for liberty from the drivers of negroes?'"[3] While acknowledging the great emancipation movements challenging empire and colonialism, Jim Crow and patriarchy, contemporary critical intellectuals have also charted in detail the ways that freedom hoists and expresses white male supremacy and the entitlements of wealth, the ways that liberalism hides the extent to which Western freedom is predicated historically on whole groups excluded from it—whether slaves, serfs, women, foreigners, or "free" workers. The movement for Black lives has this consciousness at its heart: white freedom and wealth were built from the forced labor of Black bodies and have also always entailed the right to violate those bodies. Indigenous protest movements such as Standing Rock depict white "pioneer" freedom as unleashing both Native dispossession and violation of the earth's well-being. This trajectory is richly captured in *The Two Faces of American Freedom*, where Aziz Rana depicts freedom's animation and legitimation of settler colonialism, Black chattel slavery, and global empire. In "Is Freedom White?," Jefferson Cowie writes, "Freedom was used to steal land from Native Americans, defend slavery, defeat Reconstruction, justify lynching, fight the New Deal, oppose civil rights, elect Trump and label Black Lives Matter as seditious."[4] In *White Freedom: The Racial History of an Idea*, Tyler Stovall identifies how freedom was explicitly conceived as a privilege of whiteness by both French and American Enlightenment thinkers. Many others have made the point: while freedom expresses release from bondage, it is also a language for preserving and extending white, masculine, colonial, and imperial entitlement, and for resisting challenges—from law or social movements—to this entitlement. Alabama governor George Wallace, Cowie reminds us, set loose his 1960s call for "segregation now, segregation tomorrow, segregation forever" on "a dark and visceral current of freedom as the unrestrained capacity to dominate"—namely, (Southern) states' rights against federal equality mandates.[5] White nationalists and Christian patriarchalists frame their claims in a similar fashion today.

Freedom as a gendered and civilizational discourse is as old as Aristotle's ontological distinction between free men and those nature designed for rule by others—women and slaves. Colonial European modernity had its own version of this ontology: John Stuart Mill's great encomium to individuality realized through liberty is front-loaded with a hard distinction between the civilized (European) and the barbaric (rest of the world), the former not merely entitled but ethically obliged to govern in order to improve and advance the latter.[6] He writes, "Despotism is a legitimate mode of government in dealing with barbarians, provided the end be their improvement and the means justified by actually effecting that end. Liberty, as a principle, has no application to any state of things anterior to the time when mankind have become capable of being improved by free and equal discussion."[7] Mill embodied the distinction in his career: champion of liberal causes in Europe, including the emancipation of women, he was for thirty-five years a colonial administrator for the East India Company. Nor does the formal end of European colonialism and the slave trade bring an end to the story. "Operation Iraqi Freedom" and "Operation Enduring Freedom" in Afghanistan named America's twenty-first-century successors to dozens of Cold War interventions to secure "freedom" in the postcolonial world.

Not only in our time, then, has freedom turned murderous and indifferent to its costs, casualties, and unequal applications. Since their birth, Western ideals of freedom have gifted their beauty and power to the dominant and the cause of retaining that dominance. In practice, freedom has always been Janus-faced, both the brass ring and the knee on the neck for the wretched of the earth. If today's variant especially licenses unsheathed expressions of viciousness and entitlement by the historically powerful, this may index a state of emergency for that power. It also indexes neoliberalism's unprecedented disembedding of freedom from social responsibility and from democratic rule. We will consider both of these, and their entwinement, shortly. First, however, we need to make a broader and deeper investigation of the distinctive problematic of freedom for the human species.

1. HUMAN FREEDOM

Given political freedom's abridged and distorted form today, it can be difficult to recall what makes freedom a singularly human problem and need.[8] Contemporary discourses of freedom largely figure us as on or off leash, in or out of the cage, commanded or running free—in short, as domesticated animals. This figure of us is terribly misleading. Discourses of freedom arising from histories of extreme subjugation, including colonialism, slavery, apartheid, brutal dictatorship, and sex-gender regimes, are also limited by the very extremity of the condition they oppose. At a more quotidian level, the complex need for freedom emerges from two peculiarly human features that take shape as problematics, themselves varying across histories and cultures.

First, we alone among the creatures construct, inherit, and inhabit orders and systems of power that escape our control despite being our own creation—this is Marx-Weber-Foucault 101. These orders and systems of power are often but not always invisible and unnamed, inevitably complex, and traverse psychic, social, economic, cultural, and political registers. We alone among the creatures are dominated through these orders and systems, the interdependence and stratification they entail, and not only by physical strength, command, rules, interdictions, and control of resources. We alone struggle to craft and govern lives, individually and together, amid orders of power that we generate and reproduce but that slip our grasp. This includes powers entailed in modes of production and consumption, in finance and technology, in culture and religion, and in subject constitution, stratification, and abjection at the site of race, gender, sexuality, caste, and ethnicity. Neither natural nor divine, and emanating from yet exceeding human intention, stewardship, or consent, these orders of power generate hierarchies, exclusions, subjectivities, potentials, conduct, and suffering. The more sophisticated, complex, global, and invasive they become (and this increasing complexity and reach of power perhaps remains the only way that history can still be said to "develop"), the greater become freedom's challenges. This singular species generativity, and potential for collective subjugation through it, is one part of freedom's scene—and is ignored by that figure of us as animals leashed, commanded, or free to do as we please.

Indeed, freedom conceived as an individual holding and exercised as personal choice elides the world-making powers through which we are shaped, burdened, and constrained. This is precisely the elision performed by liberalism and is what constitutes modern liberal and especially neoliberal formulations of freedom as deserting rather than culminating a long historical wrestle with freedom's meaning and possibility. Locating liberty in the individual and identifying it with noninterference from others or the state, liberalism unleashes us amid powers we do not control, understand, or often name—powers that stratify, subject, and now existentially threaten us. Blending liberalism with democracy or republicanism little tames the force of this move. Whenever freedom is framed as absence of literal interdiction, whether that of a master, tyrant, law, or state, it ignores freedom's scene.

I hasten to add that the formal equality, abstract individuality, and personal choice consecrated by liberalism are not terrible things, and we need not dismiss them to dismantle their claim to realize freedom. It is one thing to want both, another to allow them to displace reckoning with the immense powers that constitute, organize, and dominate us. Today, this reckoning is further postponed by the collapse of progress narratives, let alone revolutionary ones. As the powers dominating us increase and ramify, the prospect of controlling them recedes, which is undoubtedly why Fredric Jameson's remark that "it is easier to imagine the end of the world than the end of capitalism" strikes such a chord. Again, liberalism, far from providing means to corral and handle together powers that dominate us, facilitates our surrender to them; neoliberalism completes this surrender. Limning a constricted horizon of human possibility for self-governing, liberalism offers the solace of withdrawal and nonresponsibility for the world we make and inhabit together. And, of course, the birth of this creed for withdrawal and non-responsibility coincided with the Industrial Revolution's intense acceleration of the Anthropocene, about which more in a moment.

The second peculiarly human feature setting the scene of freedom pertains to the domain we have come to call political. As animals who neither roam solo nor herd together instinctively, we everywhere and always organize ourselves in part through arrangements of rule. (Only the anarchist tradition stands apart from this; not even the neoliberals or libertarians reject all forms of rule.) In contrast with the Marx-Weber-Foucault analytics of power developing the first problematic, this one is associated with figures such as Aristotle and Rousseau. It is the basis on which democracy—the nearly impossible task of ruling ourselves so we are not ruled by others—belongs to us alone among the animals. The political may be conceived as the most artificial of the power registers: Hobbes spoke of the "Commonwealth or State" as pure human artifice, contrasting it with the natural order generated by God. Powers of rule, whether concentrated or distributed, institutionalized or individually enacted, differ in kind from our unique capacity to generate orders of social power through which we are then dominated, though they may emanate from, blend with, consecrate, enforce, regulate, or overturn

23

those powers. The powers of rule, distinctive to political life and to us as political creatures, can be called freedom's second scene.

Freedom defined as ownership and control of the means of production, the Marxist tradition that taught us so much about the first problematic shaping freedom's scene, is of no help in thinking about it in the second. Marx was too seduced by his own critique of the state, too eager to subvert the Hegelian preoccupation with it, too anxious to reveal what he identified initially as civil society and then as the capitalist mode of production as exhaustive of unemancipated existence, to allow the complexities of political power and political rule a place in the ontics of communist freedom. Yet at what cost! Even political powers required for handling public ownership never disappear and are enormously difficult to democratize, as every actually existing socialist state has revealed. Beyond ownership, there are other powers of rule that exceed roots and reproduction in private property, powers that other radical thinkers would surface through the important yet still inadequate lexicons of racial capitalism, care work, decolonization, normative sexual regimes, and much else. On the other hand, the political theory tradition concerned with just rule, and especially with political freedom exercised through shared rule, has always neglected the orders of social power constituting freedom's first scene. This is true across the Aristotelian, Rousseauian, and neo-Kantian traditions that dominate democratic theory today. (Democratic socialist thinking is no exception, as it tends to align freedom with democracy and equality with socialism.)

This tendentious rehearsal of familiar ground aims only to remind us that the problematics of both individual and political freedom arise, on the one hand, from the difficulty of controlling or governing the multiple forms of power humans generate together and, on the other hand, from the fact that organizing political power as political freedom is inordinately challenging. Our inherited traditions of political theory have not reckoned well with connecting them, tending to locate "emancipation" in the former and "democracy" in the latter, and yielding, as a consequence, formulations of unemancipated democracy or of undemocratized emancipation. Moreover, both traditions, together with the histories they articulate, feature a consequential anthropocentrism and linking of freedom to sovereignty that has yielded the unprecedented danger and destructiveness of the Anthropocene.

The Anthropocene. One more turn of the screw. Before considering how neoliberalism intensifies liberalism's disavowals of the powers creating freedom's scene, we need to add another layer to the powers that make our history yet escape our grasp: our distinctive species' capacity to transform the planet. The Anthropocene names the power of human history to alter natural history, its course, and its pace.[9] We are the only species so powerful that we could and have become a global geological force, "changing the most basic physical processes of the earth."[10] All canonical Western formulations of freedom ignore this, though some Indigenous and non-Western knowledges and practices do better.

The relevance to freedom of the Anthropocene exceeds the matter of limits required for self-preservation, which can be addressed by expansive versions of the harm principle or concern with the "tragedy of the commons." Rather, the climate crisis and other ecological tipping points epitomize our collective subjection at the hands of our collective generativity, including the failure to realize our political capacity to control the powers we generate. Mirroring both our destructiveness and felt helplessness before this condition, Anthropocenic effects, themselves a portrait of freedom's scene, indict all formulations of freedom abstracted from humanly generated powers and their effects on the nonhuman, which is all canonical forms of freedom. These effects confront us with the existential rather than ethical or moral requirement of placing deep knowledge and responsibility at freedom's heart. This indictment and requirement are one piece of the novel challenge for freedom today. The other pertains to what freedom has become in the age of antidemocratic authoritarian liberalism, to which we now turn.

2. ANTIDEMOCRATIC AUTHORITARIAN LIBERALISM

Why the gangly phrase, "antidemocratic authoritarian liberalism," to depict the right-wing formations and regimes arising from liberal democracies today? Whatever their differences, they are *antidemocratic* insofar as they aggressively ignore, subvert, or cynically manipulate established legislative processes, attempt to end-run democratic checks and balances on executive power, seek to bend all public offices and functions to that power, and aim to eliminate the independence of courts and oversight agencies. Openly antidemocratic practices in the United States from this formation extend to the electoral process itself—manipulating and maiming it through gerrymandering and voter suppression, bloating it with corporate funding, encouraging foreign and domestic efforts to disrupt and corrupt it, challenging its legitimacy. Beyond the electoral process, political cronyism and corruption are flagrant and normalized, while knowledge, truth, and education are trivialized or demonized. From propagandistic lies and conspiracies to concerted attacks on the media, from devaluation of education to caricatured intellectuals, keeping the people stupid and beholden has become an open rather than closeted strategy. At the heart of the antidemocratic nature of these formations, however, is an antidemocratic form of governing reason, one in which justice-oriented democratic legislation is cast as despotic or totalitarian, while "spontaneously evolved" market and moral orders are anointed as free.[11]

These formations and regimes are *authoritarian* insofar as they identify state leaders with unlimited sovereign right rather than universal representation. They aim to replace democratic legislation with dictate and decree. They affirm military might, vigilantism, and rogue policing to quash resistance and secure order. These are authoritarianism's familiar features. However, in its current iteration, authoritarianism also takes shape through ignoring or subverting rules and norms sustaining democratic electoral and institutional processes. This has been the signature of the Trump, Bolsonaro, and Erdoğan regimes. Authoritarianism is, in this respect, a turn, an unfolding culture of antidemocratic arrogations of power, rather than an imposed governmental form. In fact, authoritarianism today rarely results from a direct coup and more often takes shape through erosions and replacements long and steadily in the making: checks and balances are sidelined and practices of negotiation and compromise are replaced with "hardball" practices of legislative maneuver, court-packing, voter suppression, legal overrides.[12] Law is openly tacticalized for partisan maneuvers, a tacticalization not

26

unique to authoritarian regimes but particularly open-handed within them. Finally, authoritarianism carries an ethos that replaces the figure of legitimate leadership as accountable, representative, and responsible with strength measured by the capacity to crush opponents and threats.[13]

Today's reactionary forms of freedom are not simply a "falling backward" into freedom's long historical association with the rights of the powerful, what Rahel Jaeggi forthrightly terms historical "regression." This is because *liberalism* remains an essential element of the new formations and regimes, even when they claim to be anti-liberal or are anointed as such by pundits. A crucial part of their novelty, their difference from earlier iterations of fascism, totalitarianism, or dictatorship, is the ardent discourse of personal, civil, and economic liberty at their core, a discourse that simultaneously animates their popular base and legitimates them. The freedom they celebrate, and accuse their enemies of trampling, is identified with unfettered private property rights, consumer choice, civic movement, weapons ownership, and personal expression, along with the right to reject equality and inclusion in the name of Christian values.

As antidemocratic authoritarian liberal regimes secure themselves with liberalism's prize, individual or personal liberty, it is not merely disembedded from democracy but turned against it. As freedom today is mobilized to assault democratic values and practices, it inverts the caution of conservative postwar liberals, such as Isaiah Berlin and F. A. Hayek, that social democracy threatens freedom. To be sure, anti-statism is an old form of surreptitious antidemocratic theory and practice. Benjamin Constant elaborated it to contest Rousseau and the Jacobins. Anti-statism became a more general cause as universal suffrage spread. Limiting state power avoided an overtly antidemocratic platform while ensuring that "the newly enfranchised masses would remain unable to wield their electoral power to impose democratic despotism."[14] The effect of this turn was, however, to identify democracy with the state and statism, and to identify liberty with anti-statism and, implicitly, resistance to democratic overreach. The novelty of the present rests in combining this identification of liberty with anti-statism and an affirmation of political authoritarianism that *dissociates* authoritarianism from statism. (The Trump regime's antagonism to both the state and democracy are exemplary of this turn.) Another important feature of the time, not novel in itself but important to the distinctiveness of the conjuncture, is freedom's explicit use to protect Christian, white, nationalist, and patriarchal features of society, and to attack those seeking to reform these features as totalitarians.

How, exactly, has freedom become an antidemocratic political sword sheathed as a birthright? How has it come to spur and legitimate extremes of economic exploitation, social inequalities, planetary plunder, socially injurious speech, the re-Christianization of secular orders, and the dismantling of bourgeois democracy? Draped in the innocence of personal expression, choice, and conduct, how does it both discredit popular rule and authorize political dictate? How has it become a political force attacking democracy as totalitarian and advancing patriarchy, Christian and ethnonationalism, and white supremacy? To address these questions, we need to reprise key elements of neoliberalism as a governing order of reason for the past four decades.[15] Then we will come forward again to neoliberalism's afterlife, including its cultivation of white male supremacist political energies.

3. NEOLIBERALISM

Understanding freedom's antisocial and antidemocratic force today requires comprehending neoliberalism as more than a set of economic policies deregulating capital, dismantling the social state, and privatizing public goods. It must also be grasped as a form of what Foucault calls governmentality, an order of reason that governs or "conducts" our conduct across many venues: education, work, health and social services, law, and culture. Within this order of reason, neoliberal reason disembeds freedom from the social, the domain that makes liberal freedom modestly responsible to others, and features the histories and powers establishing social justice as a democratizing project. Neoliberal reason also severs freedom's connection with popular sovereignty and thus with democracy. More than merely decoupling freedom from society and democracy, neoliberalism opposes them.

How does this go? "There is no such thing as society . . . [only] individual men and women, and . . . families," Margaret Thatcher famously intoned, paraphrasing Hayek's argument that the very concept of society is a "dangerous fiction."[16] Hayek aims with this argument to discredit both public provisioning and social justice legislation. Identifying both with wrongheaded and dangerous social engineering, Hayek indicts the incursion against freedom that such engineering entails, along with its misguided dependency on human intention and design in place of spontaneously evolved order generated by markets and traditional morality. Any interference in this order depends on limited human knowledge and an overreaching state, the latter inevitably coercive of individuals and disrupting market efficiencies and incentives. This framing of the social identifies it with deforming spontaneous orders and curtailing individual freedom. Order generated by markets and morals, on the other hand, is conceived of as emerging organically and shaped by evolution and competition rather than intentional human design. It is identified with freedom because of its source in this organicism rather than political dictate.[17] This is the framework that casts not only economic regulation but legislated equality opportunity for women, sexual minorities, and historically subjugated racial minorities as tyrannical social engineering. It is the framework that supports rejection of such regulation and legislation as exercises of freedom and restorations of social order.

The neoliberal attack on the social (and social justice) state for its faulty epistemological and ontological foundation, political overreach, constriction of freedom, and destructive intervention in spontaneous order together reveals the limits of accounts of neoliberalism that reduce it to economic policies of deregulation, regressive taxation, privatization, and dismantling organized labor or political policies of austerity. However, this attack also reveals the insufficiency of Foucault's characterization of neoliberal political rationality, in which, he argues, the economy constitutes the internal limit on political sovereignty.[18] (The state "cannot touch [the economy] because it cannot know [the economy]."[19]) The problem with both is that within neoliberal reason, traditional morality constitutes a second hard limit on legitimate political undertakings. Here, too, the state must not substitute for or intervene in what centuries of social evolution have accomplished—namely, an

29

order that regulates human conduct without relying on political dictate. Within neoliberal reason, markets and morals together constitute the spontaneous organizing principles of free societies, and neither may be opposed or corrupted by legislated distributional or other justice schemes. States may establish conditions and supports for markets and moral orders but may not intervene in their hierarchies or distributions. To do so is simultaneously coercive, wrongheaded, and illegitimate.

This makes popular sovereignty itself dangerous, especially in the age of the universal franchise, where the people in power will inevitably seek to remediate inequalities created by markets and traditional morality. The architects of neoliberalism therefore condemned popular sovereignty as illiberal and sought to pry it apart from democracy. Hayek called popular sovereignty a "dangerous nonsense-notion"; Friedman reduced democracy to civil liberties and elections; and the ordoliberals sought technocratic alternatives to democratic legislation while dreaming of constitutional protections for a free market economy.

In sum, neoliberalism as a form of governing reason detaches liberty from both social justice and democratic rule, hence from social and political equality. At the same time, the valorization of markets legitimates class inequality, while the valorization of traditional morality legitimates gendered, racial, sexual, and nativist hierarchies and exclusions. Taken together, these moves make neoliberal freedom even less emancipatory, egalitarian, and compatible with democracy than its liberal predecessor.

Softer and bolder versions of neoliberal reason have governed most of the world for the past four decades and have thus turned liberty into an antisocial and antidemocratic instrument. The consequences are everywhere today: in the open hostility to government regulation and taxation extending from Silicon Valley "progressives" to alt-right activists; in the broadly accepted precarities generated by privatization and flexibilization; in the survival mandates of human capital unprotected by unions or robust labor law; in the characterization of "gender ideology" and "critical race theory" as assaults on moral order. They appear in the phenomenon by which, as persons become capital, capital acquires personhood, gaining attributes, rights, and liberties that expand the power of its corporate form, resulting in historically unprecedented quantities and qualities of corporate economic, social, and political determination of human life. All of these have contributed to draining liberal freedom of whatever emancipatory force it once had, detaching it even from the ideals of Kantian moral autonomy, Millian human development, and Tocquevillian republicanism. Again, however, more than positioning freedom as independent of society and government, neoliberalism unleashes freedom *against* these things. Anti-egalitarian and anti-statist, freedom becomes a right of aggression against social mores, social protections, and social justice; it becomes an entitlement to refuse democratic principles and accountability; and it becomes compatible with political autocracy or authoritarianism. When this formation is also energized by the rancor of wounded whiteness—wounds largely generated by neoliberalism's global economic race to the bottom and the ensuing deindustrialization and sinking of the working and middle classes in the Global North—it can become freedom with a fascist glint in its eye.[20] Now freedom's historical arrogation by the dominant to protect and extend its dominance is brewed together with the antidemocratic and antisocial freedom of neoliberalism.

Things become darker still as this kind of freedom is dipped in the acid wash of nihilism. I refer not to the common sense of nihilism as existential meaninglessness or fatalism, though there is plenty of that in our time, but rather in Nietzsche's sense of a time and place in which "the highest values devaluate themselves"—values are deracinated but do not thereby disappear.[21] Absent their foundations, which reason and science erode as they topple God, values are devalued, which leads to their being fungible, multiplied, trivialized, and instrumentalized, adjusted to and for other purposes, a spiraling process that furthers the devaluation of values. Truth itself is among the values transmogrified in this way. Building for centuries, this feature of nihilism is intensified as values are openly branded, monetized, and deployed for partisan political purposes in our time. Strategic right-wing mobilization of "traditional values," including by demagogues and plutocrats often indifferent to them, is evidence of this point, but so also is quotidian corporate, political, and individual branding through values, left and right.

One consequence of such nihilism, Nietzsche reminds us, is desublimation of the instincts or will to power that moral values had served

31

to restrain and redirect.[22] When values are devalued, when they are unmoored from foundations and hence Truth, this lessens the force for containing or sublimating the drives or instincts that would violate them, and in turn lightens the conscience emerging from these sublimations. What happens then? The antisocial and antidemocratic form freedom generated by neoliberal reason is now fueled by this desublimated or disinhibited energy. But there is more. The powerful ressentiment of aggrieved entitlement—white, male, European, American, imperial—is added to this fuel. This makes contemporary expressions of freedom more than wanton or debauched, which was the classical liberal worry, and more than antidemocratic and antisocial, the inflection secured by the neoliberal turn. Now freedom rages against its lost entitlements and against those it casts as agents of that loss—immigrants, minorities, feminists, global elites, and the tiny remains of the redistributive state.

Freedom divorced from society and democracy, radically disinhibited, low on conscience, and stung by lost entitlement also turns vengeful and revengeful, attacking the world it resents. Responsible to nothing and no one, sometimes openly spurning truth and reason, it easily becomes furious and destructive, venting its injury as rage. This is the freedom of the Klan's and Nazis' "free speech" rallies, of the Proud Boys attacking Black Lives Matter protesters or invading the Capitol, of vigilante militias at the US-Mexico border hunting down migrants, but also of ordinary white people exploding at ordinary people of color in ordinary settings—at the mall, the park, the traffic intersection, Chinatown.[23] It is the freedom of the gleefully "politically incorrect" in both virtual and live spaces, of the right-wing equation of social justice with "cancel culture," and of last stands that can only revile, ridicule, and denounce. This is how nihilism's desublimated will to power intersects neoliberal reason and neoliberal effects to generate a novel form of freedom today. Neoliberalism's consecration of markets and traditional moral order, in place of democracy and society, are the framework. Nihilism's desublimations and disinhibitions are the fuel. The legacy of entitlements from institutionalized white male supremacy is the animus.

It is easy to see this antisocial, antidemocratic freedom in neo-Nazis, right-wing militias, alt-right provocateurs, and angry "Karens" in parks, in stores, and on sidewalks. This freedom is also embedded in the antidemocratic project directed toward re-Christianizing secular and multicultural nations. Here, freedom detached from democracy and embedded in markets and morality is deployed to secure conservative Christian morality—and repel egalitarian challenges to it—in schools, courts, and public and commercial spaces. Gender and sexual equality are dismantled not through frontal attacks on them but by enhancing the power and expanding the venues for religious liberty beyond churches and the private sphere. Through "religious freedom restoration acts" and scores of legal decisions rooted in neoliberal jurisprudence, Christian businesses, hospitals, and nonprofits have won the right to impose their values on those they employ, serve, teach, or care for.[24] This is freedom against equality, yes, but also freedom against social justice *tout court*, freedom expanded in its reach and range to displace other principles of justice. As religious liberty is extended to corporations and women's health clinics and churches win the right to engage in political activity, this novel form of freedom facilitates the project of re-Christianizing nations and making "family values" into governing truths.[25]

33

In short, in the street, freedom is mobilized as a vicious attack dog against what remains of society and democracy. In legislatures and courts, it is mobilized for the resecuring of historical hierarchies and exclusions as well as corporate power. At both levels, it converges easily with authoritarianism as it aims at de-democratizing the state. As the spawn of neoliberal reason, neoliberal socioeconomic effects, nihilism, and a legacy of freedom imbricated with supremacist power and exclusions, this formation will not melt away as neoliberal economic policies are abandoned. Policy can be changed on a dime, while orders of governing reason build and recede slowly; their effects generate their own logics and trajectories, subject and social formations. Moreover, the *political force* of disinhibited antisocial, antidemocratic freedom both anoints and fortifies a dying demographic that will cling to its hegemony with its last breath.

For the scene of freedom with which we began—in which the complex powers we generate become forces of history and social life that dominate us and in which political rule supplants rule by these forces—

this exercise of force is a mirror, not a resource. Neither justice nor liberation is available within its terms and coordinates. Rather, it offers a perverse resolution of the tension in modern liberty present from the beginning—rights against the state or the political right to the state?—by casting both as undemocratic.

4. WHAT WAS EMANCIPATION?

As freedom grows uglier and its historical imbrication with dominance is made manifest, can we even recall its emancipatory promise? What were the Western visions of human liberation from the vicissitudes of nature, need, and human powers? Plato imagined escape from the sensuous world—flight into philosophy and the Forms; Augustine gave us the Christian version as fleshless and otherworldly. For Aristotle, the elite find freedom in political rule and intellectual contemplation, but only if unfree others—slaves, women, workers—provision their needs.[26] Rousseau, also anxious about body, desire, and need, sought to extract us from interpersonal dependency and make us dependent instead on the political whole steered by common political will. Hegel located freedom in reconciling individual consciousness with the universality of the state and Christianity, a formula Marx regarded as purely a symptom of the age.

Marx—the thinker who taught us that freedom must be wrested from and through our complex species generativity and power! Freedom would be located within rather than apart from our social interdependence; on earth, for which heaven is but an inverted projection; by facing our needs together, not running from them or enslaving or exploiting a class to serve them; by owning—not ruling—in common; through substantive universality and equality, not the abstract versions offered by the constitutional state. Marx's critique of liberalism (not named as such) in "On the Jewish Question" remains unparalleled: there, Marx links the abstraction, egoism, and religiosity of bourgeois freedom to the specific powers and illusions of the postfeudal age. Not to capitalism, for which he does not yet have a name or a theory, but to the breakup of feudal property relations and ascendance of bourgeois class power. The critique rests on the distinction between "political emancipation," which may expand citizenship and rights to heretofore excluded populations without touching the powers generating that exclusion and stratification, and the "true human emancipation" that he casts as our yearning, entitlement, and destiny. After this early wrestle with Hegel and the Hegelians, his writings on political economy would elaborate the conditions for real emancipation as collective ownership and control of the means of production. Only in volume 3 of *Capital*, however, does Marx give us a glimpse of freedom's final form. Freedom's precondition, he writes, is "the associated producers . . . rationally regulating their interchange with Nature, bringing it under their common control . . . with the least expenditure of energy and under conditions most favorable to and worthy of their human nature." Here, though, we are still bound to the necessary—labor, needs, production. Only "beyond [production] begins that development of human energy which is an end in itself, the true realm of freedom, which, however, can blossom forth only with the realm of necessity as its basis." Only beyond labor is there freedom. This passage thus concludes: "The shortening of the working day is [freedom's] basic prerequisite."[27]

No grimly toiling masses for this communist! Freedom was always the essence of the matter, what both powered and redeemed human history. Collective ownership is the condition but not the realization of freedom. Lost in Marxist screeds about unequal distributions of wealth and in Marxism's bastard offspring—state communism, social democracy, the welfare state—was this: we are emancipated when laboring is left behind and we can create, invent, imagine as we wish. We are back to Aristotle, but now freedom from necessity and for "the good life" for all rather than the few. We are also, however, in the web of the modern, where freedom is about self-realization and everything else is its instrument. If Weber charted the dangers of such instrumental rationality in building giant machineries of human domination—iron cages—the catastrophe of this way of thinking is now reflected in the climate crisis.

There is so much else that Marx's formulation neglected. It did not address the crucial *political* powers essential to handling public ownership, powers that never disappear and are difficult to democratize, as every experiment with Marxist revolutionary states reveals. It did not address the powers specific to colonialism, patriarchy, and racialization apart from their links to private property, powers that Frantz Fanon, Cedric Robinson, C. L. R. James, W. E. B. Du Bois, Aimé Césaire, Édouard Glissant, Stuart Hall, Paul Gilroy, Angela Davis, and others would surface, especially through the important yet still inadequate lexicon of racial capitalism. It did not address normative valorizations and demonizations of designated bodies and desires, which feminist theory, queer theory, and critical race theory mostly had to depart from Marx and Marxism to bring into relief. It did not register semiotic or discursive powers constitutive of such hierarchies and abjections, the powers lyricized in Martin Luther King Jr.'s "Letter from a Birmingham Jail" and in the writings of Frederick Douglass, Kiese Laymon, Toni Morrison, Robin Kelly, Patricia Williams, and others—these too leaving Marxism behind. And, as it took over Enlightenment and especially Hegelian and Kantian assumptions about freedom and rationality as the engines of human history, it did not confront our complex psychic natures and history's continuous crafting of them, the complexity and crafting that throw into question both our desire and capacity for freedom, and also complicate and multiply "reason."

Early twentieth-century fascism and the critical theory arising in response to it would finally foreground this problem. Mirroring the history it tried to fathom, *Dialectic of Enlightenment* crushed the promise of reason and *One-Dimensional Man* revealed how easily emancipatory desire could be bought off and co-opted by capitalist production and consumption. Even before this, however, the assumption of freedom as an object of human desire and engine of history had been challenged by Dostoyevsky, Nietzsche, and Freud. Dostoyevsky: Do humans really want freedom? Do we prefer "bread," ease, conformity, and authority? Nietzsche: Are not most inclined to reproach and moralize, or follow the herd, rather than rise to the tasks of crafting a life and handling power? Freud: Are our instincts and their vicissitudes even oriented toward freedom? Can civilization, born of instinctual sublimation and repression, tolerate the freedom we clamor for?

Black, feminist, and queer liberation movements revived freedom talk in the 1960s, and then came the searing blows to it delivered by poststructuralist thought. If we are constituted and not just repressed

36

by power, if subjectivization designates the process of becoming a subject, what could freedom even mean? If power is ubiquitous, and not only exercised through political sovereignty or modes of production but everywhere in social relations and discourse, and if everything we do is immanent to those, is freedom even coherent? A practice, an exercise, or an ethos, Foucault says; freedom is not a possession or condition. Arts of the self, resistance, counter-discourse, being governed a little less— "like this, not like that"—these are the most we might hope for after critiques of the essential subject, progress, and utopias in which power is imagined as vanquished or radically collectivized.

Where are we, then? Freedom as emancipation is beset from every direction today. Intellectually incoherent after Nietzsche, Freud, Foucault, and left critical theory working in their legacy, how can it survive the collapse of progressive and dialectical historiography, of essentialist and unified figures of the subject, of theories of social totalities? How can it surmount challenges to the premise that humans want to govern themselves, rule themselves, even give moral compass to themselves rather than surrender to markets or to secular or religious authority? How can it accommodate post-Marxist multiplications of power—race, sexuality, gender, coloniality, and (dis)ability added to class; political rule added to control of production; biopower, disciplinary power, discursive power, normative power, and linguistic power added to "materialism"? What is freedom if we are always governed through normative orders of reason, so difficult to apprehend? And on what scale would we plot emancipation today—local, national, postnational, global?

Amid this constellation of challenges, do we abandon freedom or transpose it into a different register? Do we recast freedom as teleology into freedom as permanent project, always in process, always incomplete, and always changing its meanings and referents? That is one question at this point in the story. But we also need to ask what to do with freedom at a historical conjuncture when it has truly gone rogue, when it has been ripped from contexts through which it could support rather than destroy prospects of justice, eco-viability, and peaceful cohabitation, when the alchemy of neoliberalism, white male supremacy, and nihilism have made freedom monstrous. What is freedom's place in elaborating visions and values that could both resist these forces and script political, economic, and social coordinates for a just and sustainable future? What is freedom's part in redeeming the promise that humans can govern the complex powers we generate and not only make a grievous, frightening mess from our distinctive species capacities? What kind of freedom do we fight for now, and what kind could challenge freedom twinned with fascism?

These are not questions to answer in haste or with tidy principles. They are provocations for our political and theoretical work to come. I conclude with just a few speculative thoughts.

First, the freedom we affirm cannot be organized by the terms of liberalism. This does not mean abandoning concern with individual desires, capacities, judgments, or rights. But there is no room and no time left on this planet to be governed politically by principles arising from an ontology that detaches individual existence and actions from complex human and earthly interdependence, from the extraordinary powers we generate, and from the movement and fate of the whole. If our species mode of existence generates extreme stratification and ecological destruction, then formulating freedom as personal license is both incoherent and criminal. This formulation opposes freedom and justice, and freedom and planetary viability, and it compromises all hope of robust democratic rule.

Second, freedom must be bound so tightly to responsibility that the latter is known and felt as freedom's constitutive ethos rather than its limit. Responsibility, in turn, must be extended to intentional and unintentional effects and to all that humans touch, including the most delicate balances in human and ecological communities. More than simply socially re-embedded, freedom must have at its heart responsibility for the unique power of our species to alter *everything* through our activity. Activity, in turn, must be understood to include language, communicative technologies, production, consumption, and a range of endeavors in the domains of economy, society, polity, and culture.

Third, freedom must be embedded in aspirations to deepen and expand democratic rule everywhere—workplaces, communities, nations, and beyond. Again, this does not mean demonizing personal choice and latitude in individual attachments, tastes, life forms, and vocations, but nesting these within a common good shaped by an educated, democratic people. We have not been well served by opposing or radically severing personal and political, negative and positive, or private and public registers of freedom. The distinctions matter but should not be converted into oppositions or exclusions. Without relating these registers, we have no path to justice or a protected planet. Oppositions between freedom and equality also invariably leave the Right clutching the former and the Left demanding the latter. As we have learned from freedom's historical saturation with white male propertied entitlement, equality is all that paves the road to freedom for all. Moreover, political equality alone realizes the promise of democracy, the freedom to rule our common life together.

Finally, freedom, in theory and practice, must constantly reckon with powers difficult to democratize—contemporary material powers of class, gender, and race and powers carried in linguistic, discursive, psychic, and technological registers.[28] That such powers are not always possible to collage and govern in common is freedom's permanent provocation and incitement, not its defeat. Naming and challenging them is part of the permanently unfinished work of freedom. This reminds us again that freedom is not an absent or present state, not a principle to be enforced or a space to be cleared. Rather, it is the persistent endeavor to know, control, and handle together the humanly generated powers that otherwise dominate us, other life forms, and the planet we have yet to steward with care.

NOTES

1. Ta-Nehisi Coates, "I'm Not Black, I'm Kanye: Kanye West Wants Freedom—White Freedom," *The Atlantic*, May 7, 2018, https://www.theatlantic.com/entertainment/archive/2018/05/im-not-black-im-kanye/559763/.
2. Jefferson Cowie, "Is Freedom White?," *Boston Review*, September 23, 2020, http://bostonreview.net/race/jefferson-cowie-is-freedom-white.
3. Cowie, "Is Freedom White?," 2.
4. Ibid., 6.
5. Ibid., 2.
6. "Those who are still in a state to require being taken care of by others must be protected against their own actions as well as against external injury. For the same reason, we may leave out of consideration those backward states of society in which the race itself may be considered as in its nonage." John Stuart Mill,

On Liberty and Other Writings, ed. Stefan Collini (Cambridge: Cambridge University Press, 1989), 13.

7. Ibid., 13–14.
8. I am not arguing that freedom is an inherent human drive or desire—far from it. Rather, my point is that our particular struggle for freedom is linked to our singular capacity for generating complex orders of power that may, among other things, yield unfreedom. Our need for freedom, and the scene of our struggle for it, is bound to this capacity, not to any subjective desire or spirit of history.
9. Dipesh Chakrabarty, "The Climate of History: Four Theses," *Critical Inquiry* 35, no. 2 (Winter 2009): 197–222.
10. Ibid., 206.
11. I have theorized this form of governing reason in *In the Ruins of Neoliberalism: The Rise of Anti-democratic Politics in the West* (New York: Columbia University Press, 2019). See also Melinda Cooper, *Family Values: Between Neoliberalism and the New Social Conservatism* (New York: Zone Books, 2017); and Nancy MacLean, *Democracy in Chains* (New York: Viking, 2017).
12. In *How Democracies Die* (New York: Crown, 2018), Steven Levitsky and Daniel Ziblatt offer a detailed and excellent account of this process. Jacob Hacker and Paul Pierson, in *Let Them Eat Tweets: How the Right Rules in an Age of Extreme Inequality* (New York: Norton, 2020), also explain crucial dimensions of it.
13. Trump's capacity to destroy opponents and punish disloyalty has been the primary source of his continued grip on the Republican Party after his 2020 electoral defeat and disgrace by the January 6, 2021, insurrection attempt.
14. De Dijn, *Unruly Freedom*, 284.
15. The following section reprises parts of my discussion in *In the Ruins of Neoliberalism*.
16. Friedrich Hayek, *Law, Legislation and Liberty*, vol. 2: *The Mirage of Social Justice* (Chicago: University of Chicago Press, 1989), 69.
17. Ibid., 67–70.
18. Michel Foucault, *The Birth of Biopolitics: Lectures at the Collège de France, 1978–79*, ed. Michel Senellart, trans. Graham Burchell (New York: Picador Press, 2008), 10, 283.
19. Ibid., 283.
20. Guido Maria Brera and Edoardo Nesi, *Everything Is Broken Up and Dances: The Crushing of the Middle Class* (Boston: Other Press, 2018).
21. Friedrich Nietzsche, *The Will to Power*, ed. and trans. W. Kaufmann and R. J. Hollingdale (New York: Random House, 1967), 10. More generally, see the preface, outline, and part 1 of Nietzsche's *The Will to Power* and *Thus Spoke Zarathustra*.
22. In 2016, Hans Sluga drew my attention to the importance of Nietzsche's account of desublimation to the contemporary condition.
23. See, for example, https://www.nytimes.com/2019/03/18/nyregion/connecticut-racist-grocery-store.html; https://www.theguardian.com/us-news/2019/feb/28/how-violent-american-vigilantes-at-the-border-led-to-trumps-wall.
24. I have offered detailed accounts of this jurisprudence in *Undoing the Demos: Neoliberalism's Stealth Revolution* (New York: Zone Books, 2015), chap. 5, and its

importance in expanding the power and purview of Christian family values in *In the Ruins of Neoliberalism*, chap. 4. Amy Kapczynski, Corrine Blalock, David Singh Grewal, Jedediah Purdy, Tim Kuhner, and Sabeel Rahman are among many others building a critical appreciation of neoliberal jurisprudence.

25. https://thehill.com/homenews/administration/331902-trump-eases-ban-on -political-activity-by-churches.   41

26. Freedom, as Hannah Arendt would put it two millennia later in *The Human Condition*, is emancipation from necessity. She contorted Aristotle to formulate unconstrained thought (contemplation) and rule with other free men (politics) as absolute opposites to need, nature, necessity, and the rhythms and requirements of life.

27. Marx, *Capital*, in *The Marx-Engels Reader*, 3:441.

28. "We can't breathe." Perhaps this is one mantra of freedom struggles now. It emanates from the Black Lives Matter movement, of course, as it cites the last words of two Black men choked to death by the police. It now refers to everything from racialized police brutality and environmental racism to air thick with smoke from climate crisis–induced wildfires and the burning Amazon, fish struggling for oxygen in fouled and warming oceans, inhabitants of homeless encampments or shantytowns abutting highways and airports, and those knocked breathless by mounting debt, precariousness, and social violence.

CHAPTER 3

Gender, Politics, and the State

A Feminist Reading of Wendy Brown

Robyn Marasco

1. FEMINIST HESITATIONS

Reading for her feminism is not to say that Wendy Brown is only a feminist. Her larger contributions to critical theory risk being undervalued if measured by this term and on this terrain. Despite an intellectual tradition that takes gender and its institutions seriously and the renown of so many feminist scholars working in this tradition, critical theory has mostly kept feminism on its sidelines. And Brown's feminism poses a particular challenge to the neopragmatism and liberal revisionism that dominates contemporary critical theory. Her feminism is at odds with the mainstream of academic discourse as well, focused not on settling or unsettling "the woman question" but on deciphering a politics of male supremacy that takes form around it. Her work shows how the politics of male supremacy is shaped by the historical development of capitalism, the rationalization of the state, and the intensifying irrationalities of society, how our basic social institutions—the family, the economy, the law—are built on it and our core political concepts defined by it, and how profoundly our lives are governed by it.

Nor is reading for her feminism to impose an impossible coherence on Brown's work or the political reality she studies, as if the whole could be unlocked on a single turn. One might read her for the psychoanalytic insights, the critique of liberalism, the debts to Marx, the importance of Foucault, the concept of democracy—all of these are related to her feminism but not necessarily defined by it. The real risk in this reading is how it threatens to keep the whole of her theoretical practice bound to its beginnings. Feminism is undeniably central to her early intellectual formation, but it is arguably less important to her more recent work. Her trajectory could plausibly appear as a movement beyond or even away from feminism, away from a specific focus on gender and toward a broader critical theory. Her critique of identity politics, women's studies departments, and liberal feminism could be taken in this vein and direction. But this would be a misreading, I think, and a missed opportunity to clarify the politics of feminism.

In this chapter, I want to pull at the feminist thread that runs through her published works and public lectures, from her first book, *Manhood and Politics*, and the central debates of *States of Injury* to the later reflections on sovereignty in *Walled States, Waning Sovereignty* and the most recent writings on neoliberalism in *Undoing the Demos*. Feminism is all over Brown's work, even as she appears to move away from gender as a central focus. Feminist methods and epistemologies, those that shape her early work in explicit ways, are so basic to her theoretical practice that they can frame her later work without being marked as such. Indeed, it is her feminism—and not any movement away from feminism—that allows her to de-center gender in her research. Even more, there is a feminist theory of the state in these early writings, composed as the welfare state was being dismantled, that proves surprisingly relevant to the contemporary critique of neoliberalism and the resurgent Far Right. In the following pages, I reconstruct Brown's theory of the state—the feminist debates that inspire it, the interpretive arguments that enable it, and the importance of this theory of the state for political thought. This theory of the state shows how politics is itself a gendered practice and how gender is produced in specific political relations. It is not enough to say that gender is a social construction; what Brown shows is that gender is a political construction, upon which the state and its primary institutions are built.

I do linger on the lines of continuity in her thinking more than I emphasize the ruptures. And it may be that true theoretical discoveries are measured in the epistemological breaks—in the break that feminism had once represented for a scholar trained in the history of Western political thought and in the break from feminism that would seem to define her later work. The risk is not only in refusing the thinker the right to mature but also in failing to understand the art of reading. Louis Althusser described this art, which he practiced on Marx's writings, as "knowing how to lose time so that young authors can grow up."[1] My challenge in these pages is to show how her feminism grows up, too, which does not mean that Brown sets aside the problem of male dominance, but instead that she attends to its remarkable durability in late modernity, when we might have expected it to disappear. She develops theories of power, history, language, and desire that can better account for this durability, which also means challenging feminism on some of its core assumptions and beliefs. Still, some of her most important theoretical discoveries—about the foundations of the state, the crisis of sovereignty, the pathos of political desire, and the ruses of liberalism—are also feminist findings. Some of her most incisive and prescient arguments—about "wounded attachments" and the perils of identity politics (*States of Injury*), the liberal regime of tolerance (*Regulating Aversion*), the anxious militarization of borders (*Walled States, Waning Sovereignty*), and the odd coupling of neoliberalism and neoconservatism (*Undoing the Demos*)—are direct interventions in feminist debates and exercises in feminist critique. Even the more general features of her work—the distinctive concept of critique, the steady engagement with the tradition of Western political thought, the interest in psychoanalysis, the commitment to democracy as shared power, the orientation to history, the primacy of politics—come into better focus in a feminist light.

The difficulty with defining feminism has itself become one of its defining features. As bell hooks notes in her classic, *Feminist Theory: From Margin to Center*, there is no consensus around the term, in part because of an individualist ethos that says feminism is whatever any woman says it is and in part because of the historic exclusions that limited the feminist movement to white and middle-class women.[2] For hooks, feminism has to be defined *politically*, as the struggle to end sexist

44

oppression. This project is threatened by consumer culture, marketing "girl power" without politics, and the basic conservatism of middle-class, white women. For Brown, too, feminism is a political project, but this political project is compromised less by consumerism or even conservatism than by a righteous and reactionary moralism, an anti-politics of injury and outrage that is the opposite of shared power and freedom. Defined politically, feminism is the critique of male suprem-acy, where what is meant by "male" is a mode of power and a conduct of politics, not a biological category, and what is meant by "supremacy" is not a totality of force but the assemblage of ideologies, discourses, rules, habits, and desires that reinforce this specific mode and conduct. Man-hood is not a natural or biological fact but a political concept. Its power has representational and territorial dimensions, "the power to describe and run the world and the power of access to women."[3] Brown's writ-ings are often asking after this interaction between representation and territory, between the construction of culture and the practice of state-craft. Feminist theory *is* political theory, not quite in hooks's sense that it has political commitments (though it certainly does) but in the sense that it has a theory of politics and the state. "Finding man in the state," as Brown once described it, where we also find capitalism and white supremacy and colonialism and the ideological construction of a "West-ern" way of life, is a basic feminist procedure.[4]

Brown's first book, the only one that announces its feminism in its title, is a study in the history of political thought with a focus on Aristo-tle, Machiavelli, Weber, and Arendt. *Manhood and Politics: A Feminist Reading in Political Theory* is typical of its genre insofar as it devel-ops feminist arguments about canonical texts. But unlike Susan Moller Okin and Carole Pateman, Brown sets aside the undeniable problem of women's exclusion from this history and pursues the more vexing question of a "masculinist" concept of politics at the foundations of the Western tradition.[5] She shows that it matters as much what this tradi-tion says about men as what it says or doesn't say about women. Feminist political theory must contend not only with women's secondary status and situation but also with the politics of manhood. Today we might describe this politics in terms of "toxic masculinity" and read *Manhood and Politics* as a pioneering effort to understand its theoretical sources.

I will say more about the interpretive insights in this early work in the next section of this chapter, especially the importance of Brown's engagement with Weber for her concept of the state and her reflections on sovereignty. In the third section, I move chronologically and thematically through her writings to show how feminist arguments (and arguments with feminists) inform her entire body of work. *Manhood and Politics* comes before her serious study of Nietzsche and Foucault, who offered her a different approach to power, desire, and history; a reorientation to the epistemological frameworks that dominate feminist scholarship; and a new concept of critique. And though it remains always in view, the question of gender does move to the margins of her research when it had once been at the center. Indeed, she announces as much in an important essay, "The Impossibility of Women's Studies," written more than twenty years ago and first published shortly after her second book, *States of Injury*. A striking passage reads as follows:

> The work I am describing involves serious and difficult research, arduous thought, and complex theoretical formulations—it will not be conducive to easy polemics or slogans in battle. And it will add up to neither a coherent or unified notion of gender or a firm foundation for women's studies. But it might allow us to take those powerful founding and sustaining impulses of women's studies—to challenge seamless histories, theories, literatures, and sciences featuring and reproducing a Humanism starring only Man—and harness them for another generation or two of productive, insurrectionary work. *However much it is shaped by feminism, this work will no longer have gender at its core and is in that sense no longer women's studies.*[6]

Here Brown is discussing the problems facing women's studies as an academic discipline, university major, and degree-granting program, but we might take the last sentence as something of a statement of intent— at least it captures her scholarly life seen from one perspective. So why insist on this other perspective? Why insist on putting gender back at the center of the work, even as she explicitly argues for the opposite? Why insist on a critical political theory that is not simply "shaped by feminism" but remains feminist to its core? And how can this approach be reconciled with what she actually says about feminism's limits, missteps, and misadventures? What about her *critique* of feminism? The final section of this chapter tries to address these questions by relating Brown's autocritique of feminism to a larger set of arguments about politics, critique, and power. This autocritique could be seen as an exercise in political maturity, a virtue that Weber identifies with vocation and an individual calling but that we might understand as a historical and collective effort. The result, in Brown's work, is a feminism of strength, a feminism that defines and asserts itself politically. I see this feminism as an antidote to political nihilism and ressentiment, because unlike the identity politics of left and right, it is energized by the democratic experience of sharing power, not the sting of powerlessness. To cite her own description of critical theory in dark times, it is "a singular practice of *amor fati*."[7]

47

2. TOWARD A FEMINIST THEORY OF THE STATE

The explosion of feminist theory in the 1980s and 1990s had a profound impact on scholarship across disciplines, from literary studies to legal theory, and made such terms as identity politics, intersectionality, and performativity part of a wider political discourse. One largely abandoned part of the feminist project during this period was the pursuit of a feminist theory of the state—in the idea of the sexual contract, in the exploitation of household labor, in the structure of kinship, in male property relations, in sexual dominance and control, and in the legal foundations of liberalism. Feminists sought to identify the basis of women's oppression and the role of the state in reproducing or relieving that oppression. These debates heated up in the context of the crisis in the welfare state, the transformation of the workplace and family in late capitalism, and the backlash politics of the Reagan-Thatcher era. Perhaps the most incendiary text of the time was Catharine A. MacKinnon's book by that very title, *Toward a Feminist Theory of the State*, in which a radical critique of the state is fastened to a politics of equality grounded in law and legal redress especially. Here's how MacKinnon defends the move: "This book is not an idealist argument that law can solve the problems of the world or that if legal arguments are better made, courts will see the error of their ways. It recognizes the power of the state and the consciousness—and legitimacy—conferring power of law as political realities that women ignore at their own peril."[8]

MacKinnon's work sparked a firestorm of controversy, especially around her anti-pornography and anti-prostitution efforts, which were seen by many feminists as anti-sex and anti–sex worker. But MacKinnon's work, together with the critique of her work, also pushed feminism beyond both liberal and Marxist perspectives. MacKinnon sought to define feminism precisely as the *critique* of liberalism and Marxism, with its own objects and methods, and most important for my purposes, its own concept of the state. For her part, Brown offers a blistering critique of MacKinnon in *States of Injury*. She asks how MacKinnon has gained such prominence in a historical moment of political backlash against feminism; shows how her radicalism is undercut by a deeply conservative, ahistorical, and totalizing theory of gender; and suggests that this is what is ultimately so seductive about her rhetoric. Brown also challenges MacKinnon's critique of pornography on the grounds that it lacks any concept of representation and too readily defers to pornography as the simple truth about sex. It "ontologizes pornography *as* gender" and "mirrors the straight male pornography it means to criticize."[9] But Brown's critique of MacKinnon also points to what they share in common—the pursuit of a feminist theory of the state—as well as what is distinctive in her own account. Here is Brown, on MacKinnon's post-Marxism:

> She is a Marxist for whom history either never existed or never mattered, for whom the past has been erased and the future is an abyss, but for whom what Marx called the weight of the nightmare of dead generations on the brains of the living is incalculably heavy. As a total analysis of a social totality, a Marxism voided of historical struggle, contingency, and variation, as well as of prospects of change from within, is precisely totalitarianism. Indeed, a "Communist Manifesto" written without history or historical reason, without dialectics, without a dynamic of

change, would not only transform in tone from exhilarating to depressing, but would become an argument for the condition it describes as being in the nature of things; *capitalist domination would appear rooted in a will to dominate combined with the intrinsic power to dominate, and its "victims" would thus appear to be in need of protection rather than emancipation.* Not surprisingly, sexual emancipation is what MacKinnon is always insisting women do not need more of.[10]

That MacKinnon has no account of historical struggle is debatable, though Brown does capture the affective resonance of her work, the signature blend of "righteous rage" and "feminine anguish" that seems to confirm rather than challenge the current order of things.[11] Here Brown also explains how MacKinnon could hold such a seemingly contradictory view of the state, as both an instrument of male dominance and an agent of female protection. There is no contradiction, really, once both sides are seen to reflect what Brown in *Manhood and Politics* calls a "masculinist" concept of the state. Brown cites Charles Tilly on "state making as organized crime," Ortega y Gasset on the "sportive origins of the state," and Norman O. Brown on the "the origins of politics in juvenile delinquency," but in fact she is saying something more than all of them.[12] She is saying that the powers of the state are not found in violence alone but in the relations of (male) protection and (female) dependence that form around it. The point is that MacKinnon's feminist theory of the state reiterates the most basic terms of male dominance. Hers is a politics of protection and dependence, not equality or freedom.

Let me step back from MacKinnon and pursue the general argument. First of all, the state: "Despite the almost unavoidable tendency to speak of the state as an 'it,'" Brown writes, "the domain we call the state is not a thing, system, or subject, but a significantly unbounded terrain of powers and techniques, an ensemble of discourses, rules, and practices, cohabiting in limited, tension-ridden, often contradictory relation with one another."[13] Put differently, the state is not a totality of force but a collection of powers and practices, diverse in form and function, rarely working in concert and often in collision, presuming and producing distinct subjects. And yet there is some coherence in this cacophony,

49

which has to do with a basic political relation established by the state. This relation is not one of dominance and submission, as suggested by MacKinnon's theory at its most simplistic. Nor is it a relation of ruler and ruled, as a tradition of republican political thought posits.[14] Rather, the relation is one of *protection and dependence*—one that MacKinnon unwittingly reproduces in her presumption of female vulnerability and violability and the inevitability of male sexual violence. The welfare state, liberal constitutionalism, even the Westphalian state system, are built on this relationship of protection and dependence, on the (male) power to protect and the (female) need to be protected (from men). It underwrites the domestic politics of the state and its relation to other states. And this relationship of protection and dependence inhibits a more democratic politics of autonomy and shared power. In Brown's rendering, the state is not a unitary apparatus or a total system, but it does revolve around an elementary form of political organization. Max Weber, whose importance for her thinking is easy to underestimate, is an essential touchstone for theorizing this speculative anthropology of the modern state and its gendered dimensions.[15]

Brown turns to Weber for a theory of bureaucracy and rationalization and for a concept of vocation, but here I am especially interested in how Weber furnishes her with a story of the origins of the state and the foundations of political authority. The point is not that Brown accepts Weber's story but that it reveals the gendering of politics and the construction of masculinity as a form of political power. Actually, it's two stories folded into one: the story of the exercise of political domination (in "Men's Houses" or ancient warrior clans) and the story of the foundations of political authority (in the patrimonial household). The first story involves fraternities of violence and the forms of political organization proper to "those who have demonstrated prowess in the use of arms"—in other words, those most capable of raping and pillaging their neighbors.[16] The state, on this first account, is the lasting and durable structure that survives these archaic bands of brothers, organized into territorial units but built for expansion. The second story focuses on the father's authority in the family, his "natural" dominion over his wife and children. The state, on this account, is an extension of the "solidarity" and "superiority" first discovered in the family—solidarities born of collective consumption and superiorities based in strength and knowledge. Brown notes that Weber "largely disregards household communism once he has mentioned it" and sets aside these solidarities, as the moral of this story, too, is male violence.[17] Household authority is based in a man's physical power and his "practical knowledge and experience" of other men. "The mighty rule," Brown writes, "not because they are most proficient or knowledgeable in the realm of 'want satisfaction' or even because a need for rule exists. A man rules his household because he can physically and intellectually dominate and 'protect' his wife and children. Physical strength and familiarity with the male (violent) world outside the household or village are the basis for the household rule Weber calls the foundation of political authority."[18] Warrior clans, for Weber, are models of (male) friendship and (male) fealty. Their principles are preserved in a state that recognizes its subjects—or at least some of them—as equal citizens, whose equality is not diminished but in fact demonstrated by obedience and loyalty to one's superiors. By contrast, the household is an authoritarian and hierarchical structure, based "solely in the capacity for defense or protection against other men."[19] The principle of the household gets preserved in the state's monopoly on "legitimate" force and the hierarchical structure of its institutions. Command and obedience in the household, quite unlike that of the military hierarchy, becomes proof of a basic inequality between its members. These are different origin stories and different forms of political organization and authority, but they come together in the supremacy of manhood, the ineluctability of violence, and the powers of protection. Warrior clans develop into primitive forms of state, Weber argues, when they are fitted into territorial units and violent political action becomes routinized as legitimate political authority. And the household is central to that process.

Brown's reading of the Weberian myth of origins, in the extraordinary violence of the men's houses and the routinized violence of the patriarchal household, yields a new perspective on Weber's political thought. "Indeed, with regard to the decades-old debate about whether Weber was essentially an imperialist-nationalist or a welfare-state liberal," she notes, "this examination of what he understood as the dual foundations and purpose of political organization indicates that he was,

51

in fact, both, and on an analytic level at least, this position was a coherent one."[20] But beyond the insight into Weber's politics, which is also an argument about how liberal imperialism works, Brown shows how Weber's speculative political anthropology places manhood—marauders and patriarchs—at the very foundations of the state. On this account, "politics between men are always already the politics of exchanging, violating, protecting, and regulating women."[21] Both the family and the military appear as pillars of that political order. Politics becomes something reserved for men—and only certain kinds of men. Manhood, after all, is not a natural necessity or a biological fact. It is a political achievement. Male supremacy is baked into the structure and ideology of the state.

Brown's view of the state is drawn from Weber more than from any other source. Weber brings the many elements of the modern state into focus, not just welfare-warfare state liberalism, not just capitalism, not just bureaucracy, but also prerogative power and the gendering of political authority. Marx, too, sees the state as an instrument of domination and sees the history of capitalism in terms of what he describes, in chapter 26 of the first volume of *Capital*, as an "original accumulation" of violence. But Marx theorizes this dynamic in economic terms, and he sees the household only in terms of a sexual division of labor and the history of property relations. What Brown appreciates in Weber is the "distinctly political character" of his thinking, a quality that he shares with Machiavelli and Nietzsche and one that Brown seeks for feminism as well.[22] For Weber, the state is an apparatus of power: the power to do violence and the power to protect against it. Likewise, the household is a political order even before it is an economic arrangement. The origins of family and the state lie not in rational interests or the deliberative use of reason, not in property or inherited wealth, not in labor and production, not in natural affinities or affections, but in physical strength and the experienced use of violence. And protection, of the sort MacKinnon solicits in her appeal to the state, always brings with it the portent of danger. "Whether one is dealing with the state, the Mafia, parents, pimps, police, or husbands," Brown writes, "the heavy price of institutionalized protection is always a measure of dependence and agreement to abide by the protector's rules."[23] Or else.

From this perspective, liberalism is only partly about rights, liberties, equality before the law, and the restrained use of violence. It is also about prerogative, hierarchy, territory, and the uninhibited exercise of force. Prerogative powers are essential to the liberal state and liberal citizenship, in order to draw the lines of separation between the household and civil society and the state, to govern the family, and to demonstrate political authority. Prerogative power also makes "manhood" an essential political value under liberalism. "The gendered structure of liberalism is partly determined by the gendered character of prerogative power," Brown observes, "in which women are cast as requiring protection from the world of male violence while the superior status of men is secured by the supposed ability to offer such protection."[24] Prerogative power points to the protection racket at the origins of the modern state, where (male) violence summons and sanctifies the (male) power to protect, and vice versa.

Liberalism, then, makes an innovation to the politics of protection through its construction of a private sphere of the family, separate from civil society and the state, where (male) prerogative power reigns and where every (white, propertied) man can be king of his castle. Liberalism's separation between the household and civil society, and of both from the state, is perhaps its most decisive political act. It enables women's subjection and exploitation in the home as well as their exclusion and marginalization outside the home, but just as important is how the separation of spheres reinforces male supremacy in every sphere and gives a specific political arrangement the appearance of inevitability. We can see how liberal separation of spheres is a mechanism of women's subordination, but it also amounts to an ingenious "solution" to the problem with prerogative, its tendency to trample the rule of law and equal citizenship. Liberalism carves out a sphere where each man may exercise the prerogative power that is rightly his and that undergirds his equality before the law. Prerogative powers link the household to the state, but their separation also ensures that gendered authority gets deposited across the social field. And the household is where that authority is naturalized and sacralized. "Liberalism's discursive construction of the private sphere as neither a realm of work nor of power but of nature, comfort, and regeneration is inherently bound to a socially male position within it," and things appear different when we assume different positions.[25] It is also true that liberalism's discursive construction of the household as the place where women and children are protected or shielded from male violence is inherently bound to a socially white position in a white supremacist society, that the politics of protection is not only the basis for (white) women's exclusion from politics and the formal economy but also for the criminalization of Black men and the specific vulnerability of Black women to violence. A critique of the state must entail a consideration not only of ways that it reinforces male power but also of how it reinforces whiteness as form of power—the power to protect and the dubious power of the pedestal, of being considered worthy of protection in the first place.

Prerogative power poses a problem for liberal principles such as the rule of law and equal citizenship, but it also presents a challenge for feminism. Brown writes: "Yet because prerogative power appears to its subjects as not just the power to violate but also the power to protect—quintessentially the power of the police—it is quite difficult to challenge from a feminist perspective. The prerogative of the state, whether expressed as the armed force of the police or as vacillating criteria for obtaining welfare benefits, is often all that stands between women and rape, women and starvation, women and dependence upon brutal mates—in short, women and unattenuated male prerogative."[26] Again, an account of white supremacy is missing here—that is, how the powers of the state can be indistinguishable from "unattenuated male prerogative" and how the armed force of the police and the vacillating criteria for obtaining welfare benefits can be the primary threat, to women, men, and entire communities. Brown shows how the power to violate is the other side of the power to protect but tends to underestimate how white women and Black women are differently positioned in relation to these powers. Weber's marauders and patriarchs, in the real history of the Americas at least, were not simply men but white men, for whom "manhood" was a racial ideal. Prerogative is both a gendered and racialized power, where these categories are not exactly intersecting or overlapping but co-constitutive. Brown is exactly right: "Historically, the argument that women require protection by and from men has been critical in legitimating women's exclusion from some spheres of human

endeavor and confinement within others."[27] We should add that, historically, the argument that white women require protection by white men from nonwhite men has been crucial in legitimating racial terror and propping up police powers. The long history of white supremacist   55
violence is wrapped in the politics of protection, and Brown does not fully extend the insight and analysis that her own theory yields. Still, this basic theoretical argument, that "finding man in the state" is to discover relations of protection and dependence that undermine freedom and equality, is entirely compatible with a Black radical perspective and probably essential to the contemporary critique of white supremacy. Without it, we miss something about the nature of white women's investment in white supremacy, the roots of carceral feminism, and the gender politics of the New Jim Crow.

3. AFTER GENDER STUDIES

The epistemological limits of "white feminism" are no doubt part of the explanation for why Brown moves away from a central focus on gender and feminism after *States of Injury* (1995). The other part has to do with how poststructuralism—and the work of Michel Foucault, especially—impacted her thought and complicated the tasks of feminism. "The point is not that poststructuralism undermines the project of transforming gender," Brown says, "but that it illuminates the impossibility of seizing the conditions making gender as well as the impossibility of escaping gender."[28] Poststructuralism bolstered the feminist critique of gender as a form of power and confirmed the feminist sense that gender was everywhere and nowhere in particular, that it was both historical in its iterations and eternal in its structure, that there was no outside of the sex-gender system. But poststructuralism also dampened feminist hopes that this system could be grasped, much less abolished. It called into question how systematic this system was, not so as to reduce gender to a matter of choice but to underscore its variation in specific contexts and its diversity across the social field. Feminism was forced to rethink its grand narratives and totalizing theories, its origin stories and founding myths, including those that nourished the critique of male supremacy. Certain kinds of feminist arguments cannot—and did not—survive poststructuralist critique. And Brown's specific scholarly trajectory suggests that certain kinds of feminist arguments may have proceeded by de-centering gender and even setting it aside.

56

How do we know that this work remained feminist in any meaningful sense? Well, just as Brown once pushed feminism beyond "the woman question" and toward an account of gender and masculinity, her later work pushes feminism beyond even this terrain and toward a more general critical-theoretical practice. But the basic architecture of her early work remains. This is evident in *Walled States, Waning Sovereignty* (2010), where Brown reflects on "the politics of the fence" and the contemporary crisis in sovereignty, but without drawing explicitly from feminist sources or entering feminist debates. She invokes Rousseau's *Second Discourse* and engages Carl Schmitt at length on the question of territoriality and political sovereignty, but again, it is from Weber that she first learns the importance of territory to the state. Recall that for Weber, too, territorialization is an inaugural political act and implicit in the authority of the state. And the Weberian lesson about territory and its defense also shows how integral it is to the Western concept of manhood and the politics of male supremacy, a more muted part of Brown's analysis but still relevant to the "sovereign anxieties" that she identifies. *Walled States, Waning Sovereignty* shows how the crisis in political sovereignty has resulted in a renewal of territoriality—this time, not at the speculative origins of the state, where Weber was looking, but at its end, "at the moment of political sovereignty's dissipation or transformation."[29] It is a moment in which manhood itself, in that distinctly political sense that Brown delineates, is at stake. From this perspective, we see not only how the "politics of the fence" is also a politics of gender and how male power gets expressed in borders both literal and figurative, but also how walls could serve as monuments to white male supremacy and borders could become extensions of anxious male power. As House Speaker Nancy Pelosi remarked of President Trump's border wall a decade later, "It's like a manhood thing for him."[30]

Likewise, the critique of neoliberalism in *Undoing the Demos* (2015) has little directly to do with gender or feminism, though she does devote a few pages to reflections on the gender of *homo oeconomicus*. In many ways, these pages build upon aspects of her earlier studies of liberalism. She shows how *homo oeconomicus*, like the liberal subject before him, is a normatively male subject, whose autonomy is sustained by an "invisible infrastructure" of unwaged work that women perform in the household. She also shows how the conduct of neoliberalism, the privatization of need provisioning, and the responsibilization of citizenship place particular burdens on women. Here is Brown: "The persistent responsibility of women for provisioning care of every sort, in and out of the household, means that women both *require* the visible social infrastructure that neoliberalism aims to dismantle through privatization and *are* the invisible infrastructure sustaining a world of putatively self-investing human capitals."[31] Neoliberalism intensifies the patterns of gendered exploitation set by liberalism and welfare state capitalism. But because it sees only individual units of human capital across all domains of life, neoliberalism also renders these patterns invisible. In its relentless privatization of public welfare, neoliberalism re-centers the family as the sole source of financial, social, and emotional support for the individual left to fend for himself. But the family is also an institution neoliberalism cannot comprehend on its terms, as the ideal of *homo oeconomicus* runs contrary to the endless self-sacrifice required of women to maintain their households and care for their dependents. Women remain the primary caregivers in the home, with this work still unpaid and increasingly undersupported, yet more intensive and demanding than ever before. And women are, more and more often, the primary wage earners for themselves and their families. Under these conditions, male supremacy becomes increasingly irrational, in theory and in practice.

Neoliberal "familialism" is an intensification of the "family values" that were always a part of the liberal tradition, but with the separation of spheres now appearing in a new light. Brown shows how a neoconservative discourse of "family values" has been essential to neoliberal structural adjustment. Familialism facilitated the privatization of the public sector, the deregulation of the market, the destruction of the welfare state, the defeat of organized labor, the depression of wages, and the financialization of the economy. From this perspective, "familialism is an essential requirement, rather than an incidental feature of the neoliberal privatization of public goods and services."[32] Familialism is not simply the renewed ideology of the family or a resacralization of its heteropatriarchal form, though it is both of these. It is a mode of political organization and a rationality of conduct. It can be measured in abolition of the estate tax, the extensive affirmative action programs for legacy admissions to elite institutions, the socioeconomics of high and low marriage rates, the coordinated assault on women's reproductive autonomy since *Roe*, the gay marriage campaign, the rise of "intensive parenting," and the media's unfailing interest in the "mommy wars." The family is a basic pillar of the neoliberal state.[33]

In trying to understand Thatcherism in relation to larger social patterns, Michèle Barrett and Mary McIntosh wrote in 1982 about the "familialization" of society and culture in late capitalism. From Brown's work on neoliberalism, we can see that this is also a discernible *political* process.[34] Neoliberalism repurposes a politics of protection and reestablishes the direct link between the family and the state. The family becomes a key strategic partner in the neoliberal reorganization of the state and society. And it is among the most powerful instruments of neoliberal depoliticization. Neoliberalism expands the role and function of the family in stabilizing the economic order and reproducing its rationality, in providing for the material and affective needs of its members, and in consolidating an increasingly unequal class structure. Familialism reasserts a "natural" hierarchy at the basis of society and treats the sex inequality as an inevitable fact, not a political decision. But the family also furnishes a model of political organization and authority, for example in the gendered division between the executive and administrative-managerial functions of the state, in the basic primacy of economics over politics, and in the order of rule and hierarchy that defines the family structure. What I am suggesting is that feminist methods direct Brown to the family and the critique of familialism in the first place.

Brown's most recent book, *In the Ruins of Neoliberalism* (2019), reads as a return to the question of manhood and politics and a re-centering of gender and sexual politics in the critique of the present. Brown updates a feminist critique of white male supremacy and its irrationalities, and even returns to the concept of ressentiment first elaborated in *States of Injury.* What she shows is that wounded attachments to manhood have now become nihilistic, that some would rather destroy the world than give up control of it, and that our politics is being dominated by an especially violent strain of aggrieved masculinity. On the one hand, this is an intensification of the gendered and gendering violence that has been at the foundations of the state and its prerogative power. On the other hand, it is an indication that something has become deeply disordered in the house that male supremacy built. Under these conditions, it becomes imperative for feminism to clarify its concept of politics and its specific contributions to political theory.

59

4. THE POLITICS OF FEMINISM

The primacy of politics, though not its autonomy, is everywhere assumed in Brown's work. Her critique of neoliberalism is grounded in an older argument about liberalism's assault on democracy and the politics of shared power. But politics is also at the center of her understanding of feminism and her critique of feminism, which is itself an exercise in self-criticism and a patently feminist practice. As I have tried to show, Brown sees feminism as political theory and defines it by its contribution to thinking and acting politically. But feminism also suffers from its own impulse toward depoliticization, even apart from the general tendencies of neoliberalism. "Bosslady" feminism, the self-help mantra of leaning in, the exhortation among bourgeois women to "have it all"—all are signs of this depoliticization and versions of a specific class politics, too. But the problem of the politics in feminism runs deeper, as Brown is also concerned with how feminists have tended to retreat from power, from the theorization of power and from concrete struggles for power. It is a different concern from the one raised by Juliet Mitchell in her 1971 classic, *Women's Estate,* that the feminist movement was never really seen as a revolutionary threat to male supremacy. "It is sometimes necessary to shut women up," Mitchell remarks, "but their political organizations are never to be taken too seriously."[35] Mitchell's worry was that the women's liberation movement lacked a significant

clandestine element, that it was "the most public revolutionary movement ever to have existed" and "able, too, to make the most revolutionary statements in public without anyone seeming bothered."[36] And
in 1971, before the backlash politics of the 1980s and the virulent anti-
feminism of the decades that followed, it might have seemed like nobody
was bothered. Still, Mitchell's concern that feminism could not claim
more than a "nuisance value" remains relevant; by the 1990s, Brown
wonders if feminism even aspires to more. She worries that "we have
lost the capacity to imagine ourselves in power, self-consigned instead
to the rancorous margins in which we are at best a permanent heckle
to power."[37] Political realism is learning how to think about power, to
seize it, use it, built it, and share it. Not to refuse power or renounce it,
but to orient oneself to its demands and dynamics. Not to define oneself or one's movement by the lack of power, but to redefine politics by
the insights of feminist critique and remake political institutions on the
principle of shared power. Feminism as a political project is compromised and derailed by its lack of political realism. The problem is not
that the aim of abolishing white male supremacy is utopian. The problem is that the methods are immature.

Moralism is one way to retreat from politics and from power while
still being caught up in it. Brown distinguishes moralism as a form of
"anti-politics" from moral inquiry and moral philosophy. "Surrender-
ing epistemological foundations means giving up the ground of specifically moral claims against domination—especially the avenging of
strength through the moral critique of it—and moving instead to the
domain of the sheerly political."[38] This domain, that of the political, is
not without moral content or considerations. But the "sheerly political"
is the place where power circulates and where the critique of domination—male domination, for instance—is fueled not by righteous outrage but by the passion for freedom and real equality. Moralism is the
indignant rejection of power by those who have too little of it, not a
political strategy to build power or to reshape its basic relations. Moralism is toxic for feminism, not only because it is fueled by reaction and
ressentiment and not only for how it curiously duplicates women's historic exclusions from power. The real problem is that moralism under-

cuts and undermines the political project in feminism. The alternative is a feminism that fastens to the practice of critique.

NOTES

I am grateful to all of the participants in the conference at Penn State, especially Wendy Brown, for their feedback on some of these ideas. Thanks to Yves Winter and William Callison, too, for their comments on an early draft of this chapter.

1. Louis Althusser, "On the Young Marx," in *For Marx*, trans. Ben Brewster (New York: Verso, 2005), 49–86.
2. bell hooks, *Feminist Theory: From Margin to Center* (Boston: South End Press, 1984).
3. Wendy Brown, *States of Injury: Power and Freedom in Late Modernity* (Princeton: Princeton University Press, 1995), 167.
4. Wendy Brown, "Finding Man in the State," *Feminist Studies* 18, no. 1 (Spring 1992), 7–34.
5. Susan Moller Okin, *Women in Western Political Thought* (Princeton: Princeton University Press, 1979); Carole Pateman, *The Sexual Contract* (Palo Alto: Stanford University Press, 1988).
6. Wendy Brown, *Edgework: Critical Essays on Knowledge and Politics* (Princeton: Princeton University Press, 2005), 131; emphasis added.
7. Ibid., 16.
8. Catharine A. MacKinnon, *Toward a Feminist Theory of the State* (Cambridge: Harvard University Press, 1989), xiii.
9. Brown, *States of Injury*, 88.
10. Ibid., 93–94; emphasis added.
11. Ibid., 78.
12. Ibid., 187.
13. Ibid., 174.
14. Philip Pettit, *Republicanism: A Theory of Freedom and Government* (Oxford: Oxford University Press, 1999).
15. In October 2019, Brown delivered the Tanner Lectures at Yale University, on the subject of Max Weber's celebrated lectures on politics and science as vocation. She gave these lectures after I wrote this essay, so I was unable to incorporate them into my inquiry, but they provided confirmation of my hunch that Weber is a key source for Brown's political thinking. These lectures also suggest that Brown's own thinking about Weber has shifted considerably, the feminist critique more muted so that a partial recovery of his thought might be possible for critical theory. Here I would simply note that Brown once again turns to Weber, just as she had done in her very first book, in clarifying a properly political response to the challenges of modernity. And Brown's changing reception of Weber is yet another aperture into her thought. The Tanner lectures speak directly to this theme of maturity in politics, what a mature practice

of politics entails, with respect to the contingency of values and the inescapability of power.

16. Max Weber, *Economy and Society: An Outline of Interpretive Sociology*, vol. 2, ed. G. Roth and C. Wittich (Berkeley: University of California Press, 1978), 906; cited in Wendy Brown, *Manhood and Politics: A Feminist Reading in Political Theory* (Totowa, NJ: Rowman & Littlefield, 1988), 132.

17. The "men's houses," according to Weber, were also "communistic" in their consumption, but this point—and the connection to patrimonial communism—remains largely unexplored. See Max Weber, *The Theory of Social and Economic Organization*, ed. Talcott Parsons (New York: Free Press, 1964), 352.

18. Ibid., 133.

19. Ibid., 135.

20. Brown, *Manhood and Politics*, 136.

21. Brown, *States of Injury*, 188.

22. Brown, *Manhood and Politics*, 133.

23. Brown, *States of Injury*, 169.

24. Ibid., 189–190.

25. Ibid., 182.

26. Ibid., 191.

27. Ibid., 169–170.

28. Brown, *Edgework*, 111.

29. Wendy Brown, *Walled States, Waning Sovereignty* (New York: Zone Books, 2010), 43.

30. Rachael Bade and Sarah Ferris, "Pelosi Privately Disses Trump's Manhood After White House Meeting," *Politico*, December 11, 2018, https://www.politico.com/story/2018/12/11/pelosi-disses-trumps-manhood-white-house-meeting-1057607.

31. Wendy Brown, *Undoing the Demos* (New York: Zone Books, 2015), 106–107.

32. Ibid., 105–106.

33. See also Melinda Cooper, *Family Values: Between Neoliberalism and the New Social Conservatism* (New York: Zone Books, 2017), who draws from Brown's critique of liberalism and neoliberalism in a number of ways.

34. Michèle Barrett and Mary McIntosh, *The Anti-social Family* (London: Verso, 1982).

35. Juliet Mitchell, *Women's Estate* (London: Verso, 2015), 12.

36. Ibid., 13.

37. Brown, *Edgework*, 101.

38. Brown, *States of Injury*, 45.

CHAPTER 4

Nonsynchronicity and the Exhaustion of Progress; or, Reading Wendy Brown in Ludwigshafen

Loren Goldman

1. INTRODUCTION

Ludwigshafen, Germany, Ernst Bloch's hometown, is an unlovely city. A Rhineland port founded in the late nineteenth century, it houses the headquarters of BASF, whose sprawling campus comprises the world's largest chemical production complex. Looking northward from the city center, industrial chimneys—smokestacks—dot the horizon; swimming in the Rhine is inadvisable, for the current is strong and the pebbled beaches are all downstream of the factories. Across the river sits Mannheim, Ludwigshafen's polar opposite. The former seat of the elector Palatinate of the Rhine, its resplendent red stone baroque palace, one of Germany's largest, is now seat of the University of Mannheim; beyond lies the vibrant Friedrichsplatz and the city's distinctive Jugendstil water tower. In its magnificent glory days, Mannheim was in its own way the future: nicknamed "square city" (*Quadratestadt*), its eighteenth-century core is entirely planned, laid out in a grid of 144 sections—quadrant coordinates exist instead of street addresses. From the Bloch archive in Ludwigshafen, it is possible to take in both towns and the postwar steel railway bridge that connects them. Present-day Ludwigshafen/

Mannheim is a nonsynchronous space, comprising a multiplicity of interweaving Nows, sedimented pasts, and projected futures.[1]

I open with this brief temporal panorama because this essay is meant as a friendly addendum to a small yet important aspect of Wendy Brown's ongoing contributions to contemporary critical theory: the philosophy of history, or rather, anti-philosophy of history, underlying her critique of the modern political frame. A friendly addendum but also a warm one, in the sense of Bloch's distinction between warm and cold streams of Marxism, the first visionary, prophetic, and fervent, and the second analytical, empirical, and sober.[2] Although Brown's reflections on history in *Politics Out of History* (2001) aim to offer a "reprieve from the low-lying despair in late modern life," thereby opening up space for new political possibilities, her densely woven critiques leave hope wanting.[3] Indeed, while this earlier work concludes with Walter Benjamin's poignant image of the angel of history buffeted backward into the future by the destructive storm of progress,[4] her more recent *Undoing the Demos* (2016) closes with an explicit appeal to despair. In Bloch's terms (and *only* in his terms), Brown writes cold books. And even though hope is in many ways the obverse, not the opposite, of despair,[5] the warm stream suits it better. Using sources parallel to Brown's own, I suggest a warmer and more hopeful manner of approaching the possibilities of the future in the present.

My primary guide is Bloch, and in particular his notion of the *Ungleichzeitigkeit des Gleichzeitigen*, which has been variously rendered as "noncontemporaneity of the contemporaneous," "nonsimultaneity of the simultaneous," "nonsynchronicity of the synchronous," and "nonsametimedness of the sametimed" (each of which has its merits). This idea is meant to express, as Fredric Jameson puts it, "the coexistence of realities from radically different moments of history,"[6] and the multilayered dialectics between these different realities generate novel political possibilities as we rework the past's inheritance for the future. Bloch is a doubly useful interlocutor, furthermore, for the concrete context in which he was writing—*Heritage of Our Times* appeared soon after Hitler's rise to power—was similarly one of a profoundly felt historical crisis. Bloch sought not only to illuminate the productive power of the multilayered dialectic, but also to warn his more scientifically minded comrades on the left against ceding the territory of utopian and progressive yearning to the reactionary Right.

In what follows, I begin briefly with some of the salient points of Brown's critique of the idea of progress. I then offer historiographical comments about her account before turning in the next section to Bloch's concept of nonsynchronicity. A last section draws together some reflections on nonsynchronicity as a phenomenon characterized by standing simultaneously both in and out of history. To preview my claims, I contest that the strongly teleological, developmentalist, and universal conception of progress Brown rightly rejects is the only (or even primary) way the future has been approached in modern Western thought and offer a brief in favor of taking progress instead as a regulative idea that may facilitate political engagement. Furthermore, I suggest, *pace* Brown, that the churnings of nonsynchronous temporalities provide inexhaustible resources for political hope.

65

2. THE PHILOSOPHY OF HISTORY AND ITS DISCONTENTS

The rub, Brown explains in *Politics Out of History*, is that while stories of progress, along with the precepts of sovereignty, rights, free will, moral truth, and reason, "have been disturbed or undermined in recent decades," such stories nonetheless "remain those by which we live, even in their broken and less-than-legitimate-or-legitimating form."[7] This is not merely a problem for philosophers, as the hollowness of History's promise is reflected in the tendency of public intellectuals, political commentators, and politicians to hark back to a magical past golden age. Another symptom of this general loss of historical faith is the rise of "moralism" in politics, for when "the telos of the good vanishes but the yearning for it remains," one finds the adoption of "a voice of moral judgment in the absence of a fully-fledged moral apparatus and vision."[8] Nearly twenty years later, Brown's analysis feels prescient: in the "post-truth" era, America is to be made great (again), Britain shall be a nation of shopkeepers (again), and the "politically correct" moralizing Brown lamented in 2001 has now been "weaponized" and socially (im)mediatized.[9]

Brown thus counsels the rejection of progressive history and the embrace of a "genealogical politics" that homes in on "the conditions under which [political values] emerged, changed, and took hold, how they converged with or displaced other values, what their emergence fought off, valorized, and served."[10] To recognize the contingency of history is to realize that history is nothing but a problem of the practice of power. Freed from the Enlightenment equation of progress, knowledge, and freedom, we may then be able to "openly *invent* our political projects and their moral content, without relying on either teleological or redemptive history, without having recourse to moral or other ontological systems rooted in nature, fetishized reason, the dialectic, or the divine."[11]

Undoing the Demos presents a more dire situation, with the meager possibilities for hope further compromised by the flattening instrumental and progressivist logic of "neoliberal democracy." However problematic its underlying thematics of sovereignty, bourgeois political freedom, and epistemological and moral truth, liberal democracy is "an ideal in excess of itself,"[12] for despite its limited concrete manifestations, it nonetheless held out the promise of genuinely shared rule. Neoliberal regimes have replaced this promise with the "promise of enterprise and portfolio management at the individual and collective level," thereby eliminating space for the very idea of the demos, the platform of critique and "source of radical democratic inspiration and aspiration."[13] In light of the undoing of the demos, Brown descries the outside possibility of alternatives to neoliberalism's totalizing rationality in resisting practices of religious-cum-citizen sacrifice, but that possibility may also end up being incorporated by and reinforcing the domination of this economistic logic of governance. Picking up the thread of *Politics Out of History*, Brown reiterates her view of civilizational despair: "Most have ceased to believe in the human capacity to create and sustain a world that is humane, free, sustainable, and, above all, modestly under human control. This loss of conviction about the human capacity to craft and steer its existence or even to secure its future is the most profound and devastating sense in which modernity is 'over.'"[14] Popular attempts to resist this neoliberal evacuation of the demos do exist—Brown mentions the Occupy movement; in this specific regard, one might also include

the French *gilets jaunes*. Yet Brown finds little hope in these attempts to reclaim a political voice "hushed" by neoliberal managerialism. Her discussion of resistance ends with a rhetorical question: "A voice on behalf of what future?"[15] In the end, the only hope—and a slight one at that— 67
is the theoretical work of "puncturing neoliberal common sense, . . . developing a viable and compelling alternative to capitalist globalization," and "counter[ing] this civilizational despair."[16] While "future" is the book's literal last word, its referent remains inscrutable; hope is entertained only with downcast eyes.

3. THE VAGARIES OF PROGRESS

Before turning to Bloch and my warm addendum to Brown's critique, I want to tarry a moment and problematize both her characterization of progressivist philosophy of history and its periodization as a peculiarly modern phenomenon. With regard to the characterization of progress, it is worth noting that Brown collapses complicated and pluralistic historical discussions about its modes to the universal and steady improvement across all domains of the human condition ("toward greater freedom, equality, prosperity, rationality, or peace," as she puts it in *Politics Out of History*[17]). This legacy is of course significant in the history of modern thought; the research of Reinhardt Koselleck, in particular, has shed light on the genesis of a universalization of a progressive historical consciousness in the late eighteenth century.[18] And yet at the same time, the quality, measure, and means of progress have been contested during, since, and well before the *Sattelzeit* Koselleck identifies as the hinge moment in the development of the modern mode of historicity. Such contestation has quite literally been where the action is, be it in Augustine, Rousseau, or Hegel. In the Enlightenment proper, this sweeping formulation is best represented by the optimism of Condorcet, who offers a secular, rational eschatology that mirrors the providential and divinely guided universal philosophy of history pioneered by the theologian Jacques-Bénigne Bossuet.[19] Still, the reports of progress's supposed uniformity have been much exaggerated. The fundamental optimism that characterizes Brown's understanding of progress fails to

68

represent the panoply of sensitive and more sensibly self-aware attempts to wrestle with the (regular) crisis of historical consciousness, for, as Koselleck documents, modernity did not merely open up the notion of history as a collective singular, but also the notion of "a time determined solely by history"—that is, without reference to the cyclicality of nature or the succession of political leaders but to its own rationality.[20] As the authority of "history" grew, so did that of its authors, in both the literary sense of historiography and the concrete sense of its generative agent(s) in *événementiel* time—those who render and those who propel history. The creation of history as a problem meant that its future "opens itself as the unknown,"[21] and thus contains the seeds of regulative narratives of progress that are plural and ever revisable. In short, the transformation in historical consciousness that enables the progressivist narrative of history, particularly in its technological manifestation, also imbues a self-critical experimentalism that is only possible in light of its fallible relationship to the constructed dominant narrative of history as a collective subject.

Brown notes dissatisfaction with *Neuheit* in the *Neuzeit*, mentioning Nietzsche, Burke, and Rousseau as three rare critics of modernity's "forthrightly" progressive historical narrative.[22] Depending on the specificity of the framing, this list of philosophical critics could be expanded considerably;[23] and yet the situation is also more complicated for each of them—Rousseau, after all, the arch-critic of progress in the *Discourses*,[24] lauds civil society in *Of the Social Contract* as a progressive domain, for "out of a bounded animal" in the state of nature it "made an intelligent being and a man."[25] The debate between Kant and Moses Mendelssohn about progress is another case that shows two central *Aufklärer* wrestling with the appropriate construction of historical consciousness in light of the destabilization of their intellectual universe's core cultural and political narratives of providential guidance; in "On the common saying: That may be correct in theory, but it is of no use in practice," Kant takes pains to argue for a *regulative* assumption of the possibility of progress against the nonprogressive oscillations in history ultimately leading to naught perceived by Mendelssohn.[26] While Kant's particular solution involves the complexities of his critical system, less philosophically sophisticated contemporaneous discussions elsewhere also reflect a more ambivalent and cautious approach to history's ostensible progress: for all the nods to Providence in American thinkers of this period, *The Federalist Papers* and Washington's *Farewell Address*, for example, both present the young state as a novel, uncertain, and fallible experiment in the constitution of popular sovereignty. The hope wasn't the facile optimism that the world would inevitably come to meet us but that we could enact the principles we espouse, as guides for *our* action. I would thus hazard that a number of the supposed cheerleaders of progress in modernity are not so much progressive optimists, as Brown paints them, but meliorists who have already internalized, as she puts it, the "destabilization of *constitutive* cultural or political narratives."[27] Their conception is meliorist precisely because they do not accept the constitutive cultural narrative of progress, according to which progress is guaranteed, but rather enjoin, with Kant, a regulative, practical belief in the possibility of increasing just practices within this world.[28]

69

A second set of concerns arises about Brown's periodization of the modernist progressive philosophy of history. While *Politics Out of History* reads as remarkably prescient in terms of reactionary rhetoric and a generalized political moralism, it has aged less well in its claims of the death of progress as an intellectual fulcrum—Brown tells us that "it is a rare thinker, political leader, or ordinary citizen who straightforwardly invokes the premise of progress."[29] The intervening years have seen the rise of thinkers whose popularity belies the supposed death of progress. Steven Pinker, Hans Rösling, and the Positive Psychology crowd (re)assure us that the enlightenment (technological) project is thriving, while Ray Kurzweil gleefully anticipates the "singularity," when human beings merge with artificial intelligence; in an entirely different register, Kojin Karatani has provided a global account of historical progress culminating in the inevitable realization of perpetual peace in a world state.[30] Among politicians, the Trump administration's nostalgic fixation on a fictive past has given way once again to the usual rhetoric of progress: President Joe Biden regularly invokes the possibility that we can make "hope and history rhyme" (citing Seamus Heaney); likewise, President Obama was fond of talking in terms of the most grandiose "History," a tendency that also afflicted his predecessor, George W. Bush.[31] Brown's critique of progressive history thus has a modern timeliness to it, but it also reflects a certain timelessness to the very question of political agency *within* history that a call to move out of history cannot satisfy, one that predates even the modern formulation of the problem of historical consciousness as explored by Koselleck. The owl of Minerva spreads its wings at dusk, yet it nonetheless returns to roost at dawn.

4. NONSYNCHRONICITY IN BLOCH

I want now to approach the timeliness, untimeliness, and timelessness of Brown's observations about history from the angle of Bloch's notion of nonsynchronicity. Bloch introduced the concept in his 1935 *Heritage of Our Times*, a remarkable collection of essays in cultural criticism that links the rise of Nazism to the temporal destabilization and historical acceleration wrought by capitalism and cautions fellow Marxists against ceding the past (and the future of the past) to reactionaries. The work itself was untimely—that pesky owl of Minerva—and appeared once Bloch was already in Swiss exile, having been stripped of German citizenship in 1933; he only returned in 1949 to take a professorship in philosophy at the University of Leipzig, in then-communist East Germany.

Although inspired by Marx, Bloch borrows his language from the art historian Wilhelm Pinder to offer a way to think about the "polyphony" of temporal voices in a given present and the "multi-layered dialectic" of historical change.[32] He opens his discussion with a quotidian yet characteristically arresting observation: "Not all people exist in the same Now. They do so only externally, by virtue of the fact that they may all be seen today. But that does not mean that they are living at the same time with others. Rather, they carry earlier things with them, things which are intricately involved."[33] In contrast to Pinder, who rooted this nonsynchronicity in the contemporaneousness of different generational cohorts, Bloch sociologically grounds it in economic class.[34] Marx had explained that the development of capitalism (or any economic formation) is a slow process whose consolidation into one system of production is never complete: "It proceeds from various localities, tribes, nations, branches of labor, etc., each of which to start with develops independently of the others and only gradually enters into relation with the others. Furthermore, . . . the various stages and interests are never completely overcome, but only subordinated to the prevailing interest and trail along beside for centuries afterwards."[35]

In *Heritage of Our Times*, Bloch frames nonsynchronicity similarly, such that the existence of multiple social formations reflects "contradictions" between successive stages in a progressive developmental historical scheme. The multiple layers of dialectic enter the picture in the crosscutting and time-piercing quality of these contradictions. Hegel and Marx dealt primarily with what Bloch calls "synchronous" contradictions within a given mode of production that propel its sublation into a wholly new mode of production, "posited and growing in and with *present-day capitalism*" (32/117; Bloch's emphasis). Nonsynchronous contradictions, by contrast, are between modes of production, involving the persistence of remainders and dawnings in the social inheritance. Such contradictions are "the after-effect of older relations and forms of production and older superstructures, no matter how thwarted they may be. The *objectively* nonsynchronous is that which is far from and alien to the present; it includes both *declining remnants* and, above all, uncompleted *past*, which has not yet been 'sublated' by capitalism" (32/117; Bloch's emphasis).

Nonsynchronicity, finally, has objective and subjective expressions. Objectively, or externally, it exists in the persistence of the past's material and ideological forms, from architecture to social orders to political concepts; subjectively, or internally, it finds expression in the emotional experience of a subject living these within objective contradictions (31/116).[36] Those torn by this social, economic, and temporal dislocation find themselves, Bloch writes, filled with a "pent-up rage" (*gestaute Wut*) born of the realization that they live "in a Now in which even the last inkling of fulfilment has disappeared."[37] The upshot of the subjective contradiction is "a simply dull not wanting of the Now" that can be mobilized for any political purpose. In Weimar Germany, the pent-up rage of subjective nonsynchronism found a reactionary outlet in Nazism, built on a past of military authoritarianism and feudalism, yet Bloch cautions against his comrades on the left ceding the ground of the unredeemed past to the Right.[38]

Capitalism has the capacity to contain the explosive power of non-synchronous contradictions, which offer "a distraction from its own strictly present-day contradictions; it uses the antagonism of a still living past as a means of separation and struggle against the future that is dialectically giving birth to itself in the capitalist antagonisms." The Germans thus filled their nihilism with "hybrid structures, such as the war spirit of 1914, with romantic theories of the state and their feudal anti-capitalism, with Prussianism and socialism or other ideologies as premature solutions of social contradictions."[39] Committed to Marx's developmental dialectics, Bloch holds that genuine emancipation can only come from praxis based on knowledge of synchronous contradictions, "which themselves are the growing child of the Future or of Being-different, not with nonsynchronous ones, which as historical contradictions have their greatness behind them."[40] While their greatness may be behind them, nonsynchronous contradictions nonetheless contain a truth that should not be overlooked—namely, "that wholeness and liveliness from which communism draws genuine material against alienation."[41] Our challenge with the nonsynchronous is that we can liberate the "still *possible future* from the *past* only by putting both in the present."[42] When the latent energy of subjective nonsimultaneity is accordingly redirected toward the recognition of genuine simultaneous contradictions, Bloch believes its subjective expression is "not pent-up anger, but rather the class-conscious revolutionary proletarian," and its "objective manifestation, its objective factor is not a perishing remnant nor even an *uncompleted past*, but rather the *impeded future*."[43] The transformation of the appeal of the past into an understanding of a latent yet hindered future directs our attention to action in service of removing those barriers, toward (in Bloch's rendering) "the proletariat's free revolutionary act."[44]

For all the heavy weather Bloch makes of his stadial developmentalism in the central theoretical section of *Heritage of Our Times*, he intends his account of multilayered, synchronous, and nonsynchronous dialectics to offer a more open and less deterministic orientation toward the future germinating in the present. Several aspects of Bloch's account and his thought in general are important to keep in mind in this regard. The first is the playful, citational, and polysemous quality of Bloch's writing, which Jürgen Habermas likened to literary expressionism.[45] Combined with this is the aforementioned distinction between Marxism's cold and warm streams, or its analytical and visionary aspects, between which he shifts in his own writing. Speaking coldly, Bloch appeals to the laws of historical materialism; speaking warmly, he entertains a fantastical enthusiasm for revolutionary transfiguration. *Heritage of Our Times* is a relatively cold-stream work, unlike the decidedly warmer *Spirit of Utopia* or *The Principle of Hope*. Even in *Heritage*, moreover, Bloch offers that nonsynchronous dialectics can never be fully subsumed or sublated into the synchronous.[46] It is significant, too, that Bloch brings his discussion of nonsynchronicity back to the notion of transformation by dint of the proletarian's "revolutionary free act." Bloch's predominantly cold language here can obscure the all-important point that the multilayered dialectic is meant to underline human agency as the basis of history and empower human actors to embrace their capacity for autonomy.[47] This is consonant, furthermore, with Bloch's debt to Marx as expressed in his warmer works. *The Principle of Hope*, for example, explains that Marx's most profound intellectual contribution is his insight that humankind is the "true architect" of history by dint of its capacity to work toward the realization of a plan made in advance of action.[48] For Bloch, this "philosophy of revolution" is revolutionary because it begins "on and in the *horizon of the future*; with the science of the New and power to guide it."[49] Bloch's idiosyncratic reading of Marx also reconfigures the idea of teleology in history, freeing it from an arguably nefarious progressivism in which history's inner logic drives the unfurling and realization of a given end and in which there exists a human nisus pushing toward this determinate unfolding. For Bloch, the inner telos of humanity that unfurls in history is the self-consciousness of this capacity for freedom. In this regard, Bloch's account is teleological in that it appeals to the realization of a human essence, yet insofar as that essence is the capacity for action, it chafes against the very possibility of any particularly determinate and final social formation.

Taken in a broader signification, nonsynchronicity is built into Bloch's philosophical anthropology, for, as he puts it at the opening of *The Principle of Hope*, thought oversteps the boundaries of reality:

"thinking means exceeding."[50] Indeed, such nonsynchronicity finds expression in the multilayered temporal nature of experience explored by many phenomenologically minded thinkers.[51] Rather than remaining on the empyrean heights of German philosophy, consider an example from the mundane flats of Austrian sociology. In 1962, the same year the revised edition of *Heritage of Our Times* appeared, Alfred Schütz published an essay on the phenomenology of the everyday in which manifold temporal vectors intersect and must be negotiated in action.[52] In contrast to the realities of dreams, phantasms, art, religious experience, and scientific contemplation, the reality of "the wide-awake grown-up" is constituted at its core by somatic activity in a physical world populated by independent others.[53] Because the world of daily life is intersubjective, communication is essential to social action, requiring a hermeneutic sensibility that takes the norms and aspirations of others into account. Such meaning, furthermore, is "the result of an interpretation of a past experience looked at from the present Now with a reflective attitude."[54] Past and present are bound together, and these two are only practically sensible in the light of anticipatory consciousness: action, by definition, is "conduct which is devised in advance, that is, which is based on a preconceived project."[55] Finally, Schütz distinguishes between two modes of action: *actio*, or acting in progress, and *actum*, or an act already performed.[56] The former concerns the first-person perspective of an agent in the process of acting, during which the abstract distinctions between the various temporal layers we experience go unrecognized; the latter concerns the third-person perspective of reflection upon an accomplished act, when it may be dissected and the primordial unity of experience can be broken into its respective strata. In *actio*, temporal consciousness is of *durée*, Bergson's inner undifferentiated and subjective time, while in *actum*, it is of clock time, or objective time.

Schütz's schematization of lived reality as a multilayered process of integrating temporalities, and particularly the phenomenological disjunction between *actio* and *actum*, paints nonsynchronicity as a constitutive aspect of human experience: we are always out of sync with ourselves, and history has mostly been inscrutable to those acting within it. Case in point: once, in a fit of disciplinary oral history, I asked the Berkeley political theorist (and Brown's longtime colleague) Hanna Pitkin what it felt like to be a young professor on campus in the 1960s during the tumultuous years of the Free Speech Movement. Rather than respond directly, she referred me (nonsynchronously) to John Reed's *Ten Days That Shook the World*. In Reed's first-person account of the 1917 October Revolution, uncertainty reigns as different futures arise, pass, are seized, and are lost before the narrator's eyes. None of the actors had any real idea what was going to happen—every move was a hopeful leap into the unknown, propelled by their various, albeit here objectively synchronous, anticipations of a better world. Progress as such was neither their aim nor their motivation; rather, the revolutionary actors brought with them a multitude of imagined futures that were negotiated and reconfigured in light of events and political exigencies outside their control. As Koselleck puts it, "It is the tension between experience and expectation which, in ever-changing patterns, brings about new resolutions and through this generates historical time."[57] This interplay of polyphonous temporal voices—in the major mode of socioeconomic systems and dynamics as well as the minor mode of everyday consciousness—generates possibilities for refiguring our pasts and futures.

5. INSIDE HISTORY, OUT OF HISTORY

I question, thus, whether the destabilization of temporal narratives must spell the demise of regulative metanarratives of progress toward different possible futures, for the inexhaustible supply of nonsynchronous contradictions permit us to imagine and act toward inchoate worlds not yet realized. This is not a call for a revivification of any constitutive metaphysical history of progress, but a recognition that being out of sync with ourselves and our times is a constitutive feature of experience that provides resources for imagining and acting toward something better. As Amy Allen has argued, we should repudiate notions of historical progress in which "Reason" rules imperiously and Europe is the culmination, but this rejection "need not compel us to give up on the hope for progress in the future, though it may well change how we think about what that might mean."[58] Resources for thinking through this reconfigured hope for progress exist in the proleptic temporal dialectics of what Dipesh Chakrabarty has described as "the plurality that inheres in the 'now,' the lack of totality, the constant fragmentariness, that constitutes one's present."[59] Massimiliano Tomba, for one, has recently drawn on Bloch—and embraced the mantle of Marxism's revived warm stream[60]—to proffer an interpretation of historical materialism in light of the multilayered dialectic of temporalities in Marx's thought. Capitalist globalization, Tomba explains, not only has the capacity to incorporate resistant temporalities, it in fact relies on the co-presence of different forms of production, for "wealth produced capitalistically is possible only on the basis of exploitation of differentials of intensity and productive power, exploiting and continually generating labor of lesser productive power."[61] In nonsynchronicity, however, Tomba also finds the seeds of alternative futures: "If history is represented by means of geological layers, then the archaic, as our contemporary, is one of the frictionless surfaces that can give rise to a new beginning."[62] The low-lying despair of modernity Brown diagnoses does not have to lead to presentism,[63] for nonsynchronous temporalities harbor the hope of a different future.

The disappointments of grandiose goals, the coexistence of generational cohorts, and the multiple temporalities we experience phenomenologically—the macro- and microstories we tell ourselves and in which we are implicated—transcend our histories and point to the possibility of a fundamentally brighter future. We must not lower our sights to demand what our synchronous Now frames as possible. Prudent archers, Machiavelli writes, "set their aim much higher than the place intended, not to reach such height with their arrow, but to be able with the aid of so high an aim to achieve their plan."[64]

NOTES

1. See the feuilletonesque musings on these cities in Ernst Bloch, *Heritage of Our Times* (Cambridge, UK: Polity, 1991), 191–94.
2. See Silvia Mazzini, "Kältestrom—Wärmestrom," in *Bloch-Wörterbuch*, ed. Beat Dietschy, Doris Zeilinger, and Rainer E. Zimmermann (Berlin: De Gruyter, 2012), 224–31.

3. Wendy Brown, *Politics Out of History* (Princeton: Princeton University Press, 2001), 5.
4. Ibid., 138.
5. See Robyn Marasco, *The Highway of Despair* (New York: Columbia University Press, 2015).
6. Fredric Jameson, *Postmodernism: Or, the Cultural Logic of Late Capitalism* (Durham: Duke University Press, 1991), 307.
7. Brown, *Politics Out of History*, 3.
8. Ibid., 28.
9. Perhaps "weapons of the woke," with apologies to James Scott; see his *Weapons of the Weak* (New Haven: Yale University Press, 1985).
10. Brown, *Politics Out of History*, 97.
11. Ibid., 42.
12. Wendy Brown, *Undoing the Demos* (New York: Zone Books, 2015), 206.
13. Ibid., 207–8.
14. Ibid., 221.
15. Ibid., 220.
16. Ibid., 222.
17. Brown, *Politics Out of History*, 6.
18. Reinhart Koselleck, *Futures Past: On the Semantics of Historical Time* (New York: Columbia University Press, 2004), 36.
19. See Condorcet, "Sketch for a Historical Picture of the Progress of the Human Mind: Tenth Epoch," trans. Keith Michael Baker, *Daedalus* 133, no. 3 (Summer 2004): 65–82. For Bossuet, see Karl Löwith, *Meaning in History* (Chicago: University of Chicago Press, 1949), chap. 7.
20. Koselleck, *Futures Past*, 37.
21. Ibid., 39.
22. Brown, *Politics Out of History*, 7.
23. Including Montaigne, Diderot, Herder, Jacobi, de Maistre, Schopenhauer, and Kierkegaard. For debates within the period, see the essays in James Schmidt, ed., *What Is Enlightenment? Eighteenth-Century Answers and Twentieth-Century Questions* (Berkeley: University of California, 1996).
24. More, it is worth noting, in the *Discourse on the Sciences and Arts* than in the *Discourse on Inequality*, which allows that the early steps of humankind into society were among the happiest. See *The Second Discourse*, in Jean-Jacques Rousseau, *The Social Contract and The First and Second Discourses* (New Haven: Yale University Press, 2002), 119.
25. Jean-Jacques Rousseau, *The Social Contract* (Cambridge: Cambridge University Press, 1997), 53.
26. See Kant, "On the Common Saying: That May Be Correct in Theory, but It Is of No Use in Practice," in Immanuel Kant, *Practical Philosophy* (Cambridge: Cambridge University Press, 1996), 304–9.
27. Brown, *Politics Out of History*, 3; emphasis added.
28. See Loren Goldman, "In Defense of Blinders: Kant, Political Hope, and the Need for Practical Belief," *Political Theory* 40, no. 4 (August 2012): 497–523.
29. Brown, *Politics Out of History*, 6.

77

30. Hans Rösling, *Factfulness* (New York: Flatiron, 2018); Steven Pinker, *The Better Angels of Our Nature* (New York: Penguin, 2011), and *Enlightenment Now* (New York: Penguin, 2018); Ray Kurzweil, *The Singularity Is Near* (New York: Viking, 2005); Kojin Karatani, *The Structure of World History* (Durham: Duke University Press, 2014).

31. Teo Armus, "'Make Hope and History Rhyme': Why Joe Biden Loves to Quote a Passage from Irish Poet Seamus Heaney," *Washington Post*, August 21, 2020; cf. Seamus Heaney, *The Cure at Troy: A Version of Sophocles' Philoctetes* (New York: Farrar, Strauss and Giroux, 1991), 77; David A. Graham, "The Wrong Side of 'the Right Side of History,'" *The Atlantic*, December 21, 2015; Judy Keen, "George W. Bush Says Library 'a Place to Lay Out Facts,'" *USA Today*, April 21, 2013.

32. See Frederic J. Schwartz, "Ernst Bloch and Wilhelm Pinder: Out of Sync," *Grey Room* 3 (Spring 2001): 54–89.

33. Ernst Bloch, *The Heritage of Our Times* (Cambridge, UK: Polity Press, 2009), 22/104. For the central sections of this work, I use the excellent translation by Mark Ritter, "Nonsynchronism and the Obligation to Its Dialectics," *New German Critique* 11 (Spring 1977): 22–38; the German text is Ernst Bloch, *Erbschaft dieser Zeit* (Frankfurt: Suhrkamp Verlag, 1977). References give both the Ritter translation and the original German pagination.

34. On Bloch's nonsynchronicity, see Beat Dietschy, *Gebrochene Gegenwart: Ernst Bloch, Ungleichzeitigkeit und das Geschichtsbild der Moderne* (Frankfurt: Vervuert, 1988); Schwartz, "Ernst Bloch and Wilhelm Pinder"; David C. Durst, *Weimar Modernism* (Lanham, MD: Lexington Books, 2004), chap. 1; Dietschy, "Ungleichzeitigkeit, Gleichzeitigkeit, Übergleichzeitigkeit," in *Bloch-Wörterbuch*, 589–633; Peter Osborne, "Out of Sync: Tomba's Marx and the Problem of a Multi-layered Temporal Dialectic," *Historical Materialism* 23, no. 4 (2015): 39–48.

35. *The German Ideology*, in *Karl Marx: Selected Writings*, ed. David McClellan (Oxford: Oxford University Press, 1977), 181.

36. Cf. Schwartz, "Ernst Bloch and Wilhelm Pinder," 58–59; and Durst, *Weimar Modernism*, chap. 1.

37. Bloch, *Heritage*, 32/117.

38. Schwartz notes that Bloch is not only targeting the "left-behind" adherents of Nazism; he also "refines his terms in a way that allows him to argue implicitly against both the Second International's belief in the spontaneity of capitalist decline and the Third International's exclusive focus on the class." See "Ernst Bloch and Wilhelm Pinder," 59.

39. Bloch, *Heritage*, 32/118.

40. Ibid., 33/118–19. Cf. 33–34/120, where Bloch writes that dialectical knowledge of synchronous contradictions "activates purely the future society with which the present one is pregnant and towards which the nihilisms and anarchies of present society seek to transform themselves."

41. Ibid., 34–35/121.

42. Ibid., 33/118; Bloch's emphasis.

43. Ibid.; Bloch's emphasis.

44. Ibid., 35/121.

45. Jürgen Habermas, "Ernst Bloch: A Marxist Schelling," in *Philosophical-Political Profiles* (Cambridge: MIT Press, 1983), 61–78. Bloch, moreover, masterfully exploits conceptual nonsynchronicity, repurposing older philosophical terms in light of their potential utopian functions.
46. Bloch, *Heritage*, 33/118. On Bloch's struggle in the interwar period to adequately express the idea of nonsynchronicity, see Durst, *Weimar Modernism*, chap. 1.
47. The worry that standard translations of *Ungleichzeitigkeit des Ungleichzeitigen* (nonsynchrony/synchrony; nonsimultaneity/simultaneity; noncontemporaneity/contemporaneity) obscure this emphasis on activity leads Peter Osborne to suggest instead "non-sametimedness/sametimedness," which echoes Kierkegaard's Danish *samtidiged*, the "philosophical source of the existential idea of the *act* of bringing together different times to produce a 'same time'" (see Osborne, "Out of Sync," 44). I retain "nonsynchronicity" for stylistic reasons; for reflections on style versus precision in translation, see Mark Polizzotti, *Sympathy for the Traitor* (Cambridge: MIT Press, 2018), chap. 4.
48. Ernst Bloch, *The Principle of Hope*, trans. Neville Plaice, Stephen Plaice, and Paul Knight (Cambridge: MIT Press, 1986), vol. 3, 1354.
49. Ibid., vol. 1, 283; Bloch's emphasis.
50. Ibid., vol. 1, 4; translation emended.
51. Including Henri Bergson, William James, Martin Heidegger, Max Scheler, and Antonin Artaud, to name but a few. The art historian Pinder translates his abstract theory of nonsynchronicity into "vital language" in the following way: "Each person lives with those of the same age [*Gleichaltrigen*] and those of different ages in an abundance of simultaneous possibilities. For each person, the same time is a different time, namely *an era different from itself*, that they only share with others of the same age" (emphasis in original); see Pinder, *Das Problem der Generation* (Berlin: Frankfurter Verlags-Anstalt, 1926), 20.
52. Alfred Schütz, "On Multiple Realities," in *Collected Papers*, vol. 1: *The Problem of Social Reality* (The Hague: Martinus Nijhoff, 1962), 230.
53. Schütz, "On Multiple Realities," 223.
54. Ibid., 210.
55. Ibid., 211.
56. Ibid., 214.
57. Koselleck, *Futures Past*, 262.
58. Amy Allen, *The End of Progress* (New York: Columbia University Press, 2016), 226.
59. Dipesh Chakrabarty, *Provincializing Europe* (Princeton: Princeton University Press, 2000), 243.
60. Massimiliano Tomba, *Marx's Temporalities* (Leiden: Brill, 2012), vii.
61. Ibid., 145.
62. Ibid., 177.
63. See François Hartog, *Regimes of Historicity* (New York: Columbia University Press, 2015), 18.
64. Niccolò Machiavelli, *The Prince*, translated by Harvey Mansfield (Chicago: University of Chicago Press, 1998), 22.

79

CHAPTER 5

Voluntary Subordination

Neoliberal Freedom and Its *Femina Domestica*

Eduardo Mendieta

1. INTRODUCTION

On April 9, 2019, PBS aired the first part of a two-part documentary curated by Henry Louis Gates Jr. on the Reconstruction period. The focus of the documentary, as well as the book that goes along with it, *Stony the Road: Reconstruction, White Supremacy, and the Rise of Jim Crow*,[1] is the so-called Reconstruction Amendments to the Constitution, in particular the Thirteenth and Fourteenth Amendments, as well as the reactions and backlash against the inclusion of Blacks in the political self-legislation of the nation. In the first part of the documentary, Bryan Stevenson, the founder of the Equal Justice Initiative and the National Memorial for Peace and Justice, also known as the Lynching Memorial, is shown leading Gates through the memorial. The lynching of Black Americans became a national epidemic that left thousands of victims, many of them still unknown. Lynching, however, was not simply part of the backlash against the enfranchisement of Blacks; it was above all a form of public violence perpetrated by whites on Blacks that was meant to terrorize them into subordination. With *Plessy v. Ferguson*, this will to subordinate recently freed Blacks turned into new forms of segregation and disenfranchisement. Listening to Gates on NPR talking about his documentary and book led me to recall Ta-Nehisi Coates's last two essays from *The Atlantic*, "My President Was Black" and "The First White President," now collected in Coates's *We Were Eight Years in Power: An American Tragedy*.[2] The last essay interprets Trump's ascendancy to the White House as an expression of white America's backlash against the eight years of Obama's presidency. I must quote Coates:

> Replacing Obama is not enough—Trump has made the negation of Obama's legacy the foundation of his own. And this too is whiteness. "Race is an idea, not a fact," writes the historian Nell Irvin Painter, and essential to the construct of a "white race" is the idea of not being a [N-word]. Before Barack Obama, a [N-word] could be manufactured out of Sister Souljahs, Willie Hortons, Dusky Sallys, and Miscegenation Balls. But Donald Trump arrived in the wake of something more potent—an entire [N-word] presidency with [N-word] health care, [N-word] climate accords, [N-word] justice reform that could be targeted for destruction, that could be targeted for redemption, thus reifying the idea of being white. Trump truly is something new— the first president whose entire political existence hinges on the fact of a black president. And so it will not suffice to say Trump is a white man like all the others who rose to become president. He must be called by his correct name and rightful honorific— America's first white president.[3]

In this passage I think Coates consummately captures the racial rancor and ressentiment that propelled Trump into the presidency and fueled his administration obsessively beyond all calculus and reason. How did we get to this situation, after half a century of civil rights activism and the education of the American citizenry by waves and waves of critiques of US racism and white supremacy?

Eric Foner's massive history of the Reconstruction period carries the subtitle "America's Unfinished Revolution, 1863–1877."[4] In light of the Black Laws (those laws that were legislated after the Reconstruction to penalize and criminalize recently freed Blacks), *Plessy v. Ferguson*, the rise of the Ku Klux Klan, and the unleashing of genocidal violence against

Black Americans, it would be more appropriate to say "The Counter-revolution of White America." Trumpism is part of a counterrevolution that has been going on since the end of the Reconstruction years.

82   I have begun my chapter on Wendy Brown's extraordinary corpus by recalling the Reconstruction period and Obama's presidency, together with their respective backlashes, as a way of putting on the table a series of questions that I think run through Brown's work like arteries, supplying it with blood and oxygen. First, there is the question of how we make sense of this history, from the Civil War, the Emancipation Proclamation, and the short-lived period of Reconstruction, which gave us two of the most important, if fraught, amendments to the Constitution. This is a question of history and political agency, or rather, how we make sense of political agency across history. This question falls under what Brown calls in an early essay "genealogical politics." Second, while Donald Trump represents a reaffirmation of white supremacy and the ascendancy to the White House of a candidate who explicitly and emphatically campaigned on racist themes, he is also a manifestation of neoliberal rationality. As a millionaire whose wealth was attained through real estate speculation and the extraction of capital through bankruptcies, he is a poster child of neoliberal rapacity. If there is anyone who has contributed substantively to a critique of neoliberalism's vanquishing of democratic politics, it is surely Wendy Brown. These issues fall under her sustained analysis of what she calls the neoliberal revolution. Third and finally, as we think about the effects of neoliberalism on our political vernaculars, and not simply how it challenges the basic categories of various civil rights movements, we have to ask what happens to gender as a basic category of democratic struggles in the twenty-first century. The chapter thus ends with a close look at the *femina domestica* of neoliberalism. This issue falls under what Brown calls the "gendered and gendering" dimension of neoliberalism.

2. ON GENEALOGICAL POLITICS

In her 1998 essay "Thinking Without Banisters: Genealogical Politics in Nietzsche and Foucault," now included in *Politics Out of History*, Brown begins with the reflection that a politics guided by the modality of conviction is inimical to and in fact "at odds with democratic deliberation."[5] Conviction, as the "consummate performative speech act,"[6] collapses democratic deliberation into discourses of either Truth or Principle. In both cases, the results are either totalitarianism or absolutism. Either certain principles must be imposed or no other moral alternatives are to be considered. Brown turns to the method of genealogy as formulated by Nietzsche and expanded by Foucault in order to elucidate a politics that may be animated and guided by a different set of principles that are more in tune with deliberative democracy. The point of departure for Brown's articulation of what is at stake in Nietzsche's formulation of genealogy is evidently *On the Genealogy of Morality* from 1887.[7] In this generative text, Nietzsche's goal is to historicize our values in order to denaturalize them. Like Brecht's *Verfremdungseffekt* (estrangement effect), the goal of genealogy is to make ourselves strangers to ourselves and thus able to distance ourselves from the values to which we are attached as though they are both natural and historically fated. Most important, the very contingency of the values that orient us must be made transparent as having a value to *us*. Our values have value to us, but we do not ask, What is the value that a certain value has for us and for what reasons, and for whom are these values either essential or sacred? For whom and why do certain values count as norms and principles? The goal of genealogy, as a critique of morality, is to render legible the interestedness and partiality of moral values. As Nietzsche put it: "The value of these values themselves [pity, honor, guilt, etc.] must first be called into question—and for that there is need of a knowledge of the conditions and circumstances in which they grew; under which they evolved and changed, a knowledge of the kind that has never yet existed or even been desired."[8] Genealogy generates this kind of knowledge, and if it did not exist, it would be necessary to ask, Why was this knowledge not wanted, or why was it suppressed? The will to a knowledge that did not exist and may have been suppressed reveals that knowledge and power are entangled. Power generates or suppresses knowledge, and knowledge circulates and animates power; genealogy thus turns into a critique of knowledge. This is what Michel Foucault will take away from and make explicit in Nietzsche's version of genealogy.

83

Foucault, however, did more than provide an exegesis of Nietzsche. Foucault elevated genealogy to a major philosophical method, at the heart of which is the imperative to historicize *everything*, including history itself. If the aim of genealogy is to denaturalize by historicizing and historicizing is an effect of a form of power or resistance to it, then history itself is a value that has a value.[9] History itself is caught in the fray of power. History, to use a Foucauldian expression, is a surface on which power inscribes its effect, but it is also the means for countering those very inscriptions. History is not driven by a telos, as Kant and Hegel would have us think. Foucauldian genealogy, instead, teaches us that history is written by the victors, but at the same time, muffled but still audible, can be heard as the cacophony of the counternarratives that challenge the history of the victors. As Brown puts it, "The content, the lived modality, of 'effective history' is politics, and the moving force of this history is an often diffused, sometimes institutionalized, sometimes sublimated will to power. Put the other way around, there are *no nonpolitical moments in genealogical history.*"[10]

Brown's reference to effective history picks up on the following quote from Foucault: "History becomes 'effective' to the degree that it introduces discontinuities into our very being—as it divides our emotions, dramatizes our instincts, multiplies our body and sets it against itself. 'Effective' history deprives the self of the reassuring stability of life and nature, and will not permit itself to be transported by a voiceless obstinacy towards a millennial ending."[11] Foucault's critique of history, like Nietzsche's critique of morality, disrupts the comfortableness with the very being into which we have made ourselves contingently through countless acts of domination and insubordination, but it also breaks the logic of teleology, the logic that history has an aim and a meaning that is secured by the ineluctable nearing to that telos. To use the language of Nietzsche's essay "On the Advantages and Disadvantages of History for Life," Foucault's genealogical critique of history and its mobilization against the givenness of ourselves is a disavowal of antiquarian, critical, and monumental histories.[12] The point is not simply to generate histories, but to dissect the present, to open up the present, to articulate it as the site of a clearing in which we are gathering to determine who we have become and who we want to make ourselves into instead.

Rather than asking what preceded this moment and what will necessarily follow it, effective or genealogical history asks, "What is happening today?" This question is answered by Foucault with the invocation of a new terminology. What genealogy pursues is an "ontology of the present," which turns out to be an "ontology of ourselves." Most tellingly, Foucault places Hegel, Nietzsche, Weber, and the Frankfurt School as his predecessors in the quest for an "ontology of the present."[13]

85

Here I shall insert a parenthesis. When Brown wrote her essay on "genealogical politics" in the late 1990s, we did not yet have available Foucault's Collège de France lecture courses, and thus there was no way to have a bird's-eye view of his shifting lexicon at that time. From the 1960s through the mid-1970s, the language that guides Foucault's thinking is that of archaeology. Beginning in the mid-1970s, approximately, he adopts the language of genealogy, in what one could call his Nietzschean turn. From the early 1980s until the end of his life, he employs the language of ontology and hermeneutics. It can be shown that genealogy gives way to ontology and then to the "hermeneutics of the subject." The question of the ontology of the present, which is an ontology of ourselves, will be transformed into the question of the hermeneutics of the self, or what he calls the practices of the self, or technologies of the self, which, as we know from the lecture course from 1981/2, were focused on *ethopoesis* and the technologies of the self.[14] The point of this parenthesis is to underscore that the shift from the language of genealogy to that of ontology and hermeneutics also marks a shift from an analysis of the historization of history—that is, of an archaeology of history as the site of a war—to an analysis of subject formation, of the practices of the self, of technologies of the self. The shift, in short, is toward what Foucault calls the ways in which we "constitute ourselves as moral agents."[15]

Returning to Brown, I want to foreground what this shift in lexicons in Foucault means for her. The language of ontology leads Brown to note that "the goal is an understanding of the historical composition of our being. An appreciation of the capacity of history to produce *ontoi* (which could be translated as different ways of being in community), an insistence that history *and* man lack constants, makes it possible to grasp at least partially the constituent elements of our time, to grasp the constituent conditions of ourselves."[16] Here, philosophy becomes thoroughly historical. Curiously, one cannot but recall Hegel's statement from the preface to *Elements of the Philosophy of Right* that "philosophy, too, is *its own time comprehended in thoughts.*"[17] Genealogy turns philosophy into a quest after our historical being at the moment it is being thought. We ought not, however, lose sight of the critical aim of both genealogy and ontology, which is to illuminate how the present is always already a site of confrontation, insurrection, subordination, or resistance.

This reconstruction of Foucault's retooling of Nietzschean genealogy into a critical ontology of the present and ourselves, however, brings Brown to the following important, and for her ends decisive, aim: namely, to demonstrate how genealogical politics is a better way to frame deliberative democracy. As Brown puts it, "Genealogy's refiguring of philosophy and history extends to a refiguring of *the political* that directly opposes this term to conventional understandings of politicization on one side and policy on the other."[18] I take it that what Brown is saying here is that Foucauldian genealogy, which reconfigures philosophy into a historical ontology and history into the site of the production of our very being, entails the rethinking of the political *tout court*. Just as history has no finality, no motor driving it, as Brown notes, politics as such has no finality, no end. Or rather, politics as the activation of the political is what is at stake in an "ontology of the present." Or, in an alternative formulation: the political itself has a genealogy. In order to make this more legible, Brown then foregrounds Foucault's own pejorative linking of politicization to totalization, which thwarts the generative openness of his own genealogical investigation that resists and challenges all forms of closure and finality. So, Foucault's inchoate pluralization of the *ontoi* of human historical making leads to an openness of the political as such that resists any attempt to politicize one particular policy aim or goal into political confrontation. Genealogical politics is not just a negative or deconstructive project; it is also a positive and future-oriented one. It is the post-teleological exercise of the vocation to generate hope and open up the future to new acts of creativity.

The pivot of Brown's reconstruction of Foucault's genealogical politics is "fracture." Genealogy fractures the continuum of history: it breaks its verity; it cracks history open to reveal the "present to be the consequence of a history fraught with accidents, haphazard conflicts;

86

and unrelated events that are themselves singularly random and nothing more than 'the reversal of a relationship of forces.'"[19] As Brown observes, however, this genealogical fracturing has an entailment: "Genealogy thus *reduces the political need for progressive history* as the only source of movement away from the present even as it eliminates the grounds for such a history. Similarly, genealogy *reduces the political need for total revolution* even as it eliminates the possibility of such revolution by depriving the present of the status of a seamless totality, revolution's critical object."[20] It could be said that in this reading genealogy is both anti-progressive and anti-revolutionary. Genealogies deprive history of a teleology as well as of a putative unity that would make it the site of a total revolution. This reading reminds me of a remark Foucault made during an interview conducted in March 1977 with Bernard-Henri Lévy: "What concerns us today, as you know, is whether revolution is desirable."[21] In the same interview, Foucault goes on to consider the possible abolition of politics as such were revolution to open up the whole field of the political. Total revolution in the name of the political may turn out to be the abolition of politics by revolution.

Be that as it may, Brown's reconstruction and creative rereading of both Nietzsche and Foucault had the goal of making plausible and perhaps persuasive the argument that genealogical politics is "an alternative ground for generating political aims—a ground that, unlike conviction, embraces the contingent elements of political life and also faces forthrightly the relative arbitrariness of political values."[22] She returns to this aim by focusing on the nonnecessary correlation between Foucault's political positions and his genealogical investigations, and more broadly, on the contingent relationship between the genealogical critique of the present and political entailments.[23] In this way, one possible conclusion is that the political field is opened up to contestation but no necessary political entailments are thus derived or assumed.

To say the least, Brown's reconstruction is riveting, but it also invites looks of perplexity and all kinds of questions. If one of the goals of Foucauldian-inflected political genealogy is to reduce the need for both progressive history and revolution, one question arises immediately— that is, on what grounds are we to challenge a particular presentation of the historical ontology of ourselves that may lead to an efficacious history? If the aim is to mobilize the present in a certain direction, we have to persuade others to push history in that direction, a direction that we project as one that we can sketch collectively. And on what grounds can we persuade them to push in that direction, once we have persuaded them of the artificiality of what we take to be immutable and the truth of history? I think it was Ernst Bloch, arguing against György Lukács, who said that one's aesthetics do not determine one's politics; one could be for surrealism and expressionism and still subscribe to right-wing politics. I do not think this applies to the relationship between genealogical critiques and political entailments: the aim of such genealogical critiques is to liberate us to other possible versions of ourselves, versions that we project in the name of making ourselves better and not simply different. To return to my introduction, part of the challenge with Trumpism is that it is mobilizing its own type of genealogical politics, one in the service of a certain portrait of the United States that is captured in its retrograde and regressive slogan "Make America Great Again." For whom, when, how, was "America Great"? Neoliberal authoritarianism and white supremacist politics are also mobilizing their own version of history. They also have a version of their "better." This, then, raises the question as to "better" in what sense, or how, or as against what, and for whom?

Genealogical politics do fracture and disrupt how we perceive and represent ourselves, as well as providing us with new vocabularies to talk about what the political is. In fact, one of the gains of Brown's articulation of genealogical politics is to show how the critiques enabled by such genealogies are the opening up of the political as such—that is, that fields of human interaction that were consigned to the realm of the private can now be articulated as belonging to the political field. If the political as such can become a genealogical object, this means it can also be destabilized and denaturalized; the political then becomes part of the ontology of the present. Yet the gains of genealogical politics cannot be as anodyne as claiming that by opening the horizon of the political we can talk about ourselves differently. There is a difference that makes a difference, and that difference is one that can and should make a difference in moving us in a deliberately different direction, one that we can persuade each other as being worth pursuing.

Habermas accused Foucault of crypto-normativism, of subscribing to a concealed or hidden set of norms that oriented both his deconstructive genealogies but also his own political projects and interventions. I think that Brown's own crypto-normativism is unmasked in her work on neoliberalism and the powerful opening chapter of the present book.

3. THE NEOLIBERAL EVISCERATION OF DEMOCRATIC POLITICS

Brown's 2015 book *Undoing the Demos: Neoliberalism's Stealth Revolution* provides not only one of the most comprehensive critiques of neoliberalism that has been written, but also a substantive reconstruction of Foucault's analysis of the rise of neoliberalism that is at the same time a critique that takes us beyond Foucault's own genealogy of neoliberalism.[24] At the heart of Brown's genealogy of neoliberalism, via Foucault, is the critique and deconstructive unmasking of the ways in which neoliberalism's reduction of social agents and citizens to *homo oeconomicus* has brought about the usurpation of *homo politicus*. In fact, the sequestration of the latter by the former has meant the eclipse of what Brown calls democratic imaginaries. This eclipse, furthermore, has meant the closure of horizons of collective action and thus of democratic self-legislation. Still, at the outset I choose to focus on Brown's important discussion of the relationship between the ascendancy of *homo oeconomicus* and what she calls the *femina domestica*, or the condition of possibility of the very ascendancy of *homo oeconomicus*.

The pedestrian or average understanding of neoliberalism usurps and shifts the logic of liberalism. If liberalism focused on rights and the state as a regulator of markets, neoliberalism focuses on freedom of commerce and the extrication of the state from the regulation of the market. If liberalism spoke for regulation, neoliberalism speaks for deregulation. If liberalism sought to guide the invisible hand of the market through policies, neoliberalism frees the market's hand absolutely. Absolutely free markets are putatively the most absolute form of freedom. This has become a new gospel, and its theology is the complete deregulation of the markets. If capitalism secures freedom, as Milton Friedman argued, absolutely deregulated markets are the vitality of capitalism. This has led, however, to several negative and detrimental consequences. First, critics counter, the absolute freedom of markets has exacerbated inequalities; the economic inequality between the top earners and those at the bottom has increased obscenely. Second, anything and everything has been commercialized, resulting in the undignifying marketization of humans. Third, with the growing commercialization of every activity there is a growing entanglement among corporate and finance capital and the state; while corporate influence on the state is not new, we are witnessing an unprecedented role of the corporate and financial sectors in the very running of the state. Fourth and finally, neoliberalism instigates economic havoc from which financial investors and capitalists benefit; this is what Naomi Klein has called the shock doctrine.[25] In sum, as Brown puts it, the consequences of neoliberal policies are: "intensified inequality, crass commodification and commerce, ever growing corporate influence in government, economic havoc and instability."[26]

A detailed discussion of Brown's exegesis of Foucault's *Birth of Biopolitics* is beyond the scope of this chapter; it would be useful, however, to at least note the key rubrics or headings of Foucault's account of the ascendancy of neoliberalism.

Competition as nonnatural: In fact, the function of markets is to energize competition; unregulated market competition means healthy markets.

The economization of state and social policy: Social policy should be in accord with economic policy.

Competition replaces exchange, inequality replaces equality.

Human capital replaces labor.

Entrepreneurship replaces production.

The economization and tacticalization of law: Juridification is subordinated to marketization (i.e., law is made to serve the economy and not the polity or the democratization of the state).

The market becomes the site of veridiction (the production of certain truths about ourselves and our milieu): The market as truth; responsibilizing the state. (Here I should note that this rubric is not clear to me for reasons that I will discuss later on.)

Political consensus replaces individuation and political contestation.[27]

Brown is the first to note that this list of the key features of Foucault's analysis of neoliberalism does not do justice to his subtle and historically backed genealogies. What is important here is that Foucault is
arguing that neoliberalism is more than the transformation of liberalism into a theology of free markets, one that replaces political individualism with economic individualism. What is at the heart of Foucault's
analytics of neoliberalism is the unfolding of a new and revolutionary
"political rationality." Foucault's genealogy of neoliberalism is a "critique of political reason" as it is configured in the second half of the
twentieth century. Notwithstanding Brown's generous reconstruction
and summary of Foucault's analytics of neoliberalism, she also points
out what Foucault could not anticipate or see: the reach and depth of
the neoliberal revolution that was taking place during his own time, or
at the very least, during the mid-seventies when he undertook an analysis of neoliberalism in his Collège de France lectures. Brown lists twelve
significant consequences of the financialization of markets and the rise
of derivatives and hedge funds, which constitute the financialization of
finance or the marketization of bets on markets.

Yet Brown is interested in thinking both with and against Foucault's
ambivalent critique of the political rationality that neoliberalism config-
ures. Foucault's concern with the "birth of biopolitics," the title under
which these lectures were delivered, creates a frame that forecloses or is
inattentive to the devastating ways in which neoliberalism has affected
"social life, culture, subjectivity, and above all, politics."[28] The focus on
biopolitics and governance results in limitations on Foucault's "formulation of the political."[29] What this means more specifically is that Foucault seems not to account for the ways in which neoliberalism affects
"political life and citizenship,"[30] or even more concretely, the ways in
which neoliberalism as a "new" form of political reason impacts and
perhaps even eviscerates a "democratic imaginary."[31]

These are important issues, which I think Brown herself partly
answers in *Undoing the Demos* when she writes, "In the neoliberal *political* imaginary that has taken a responsibilized turn, we are no longer creatures of moral autonomy, freedom, or equality. We no longer
choose our ends or the means to them. We are no longer even creatures of interest relentlessly seeking to satisfy ourselves. In this respect,

the construal of *homo oeconomicus* as human capital leaves behind not only *homo politicus* but humanism itself" (41–42). The neoliberal political imaginary has turned us into hedge funds that are beyond ethics, political equality, and of course political freedom. The political imaginary of neoliberalism is the refutation of humanism and the reintroduction of the state of nature into the very heart of the social contract. As Brown notes, neoliberalism inverts the passage from the state of nature into the social compact. As pure economic creatures, we are now in the brutal utopia of the state of nature as the absolute freedom of markets. I would think of neoliberal marketization and financialization of our entire social life as the unmooring of the panopticon into the very core of the fabric of sociality, where it is no longer a peripheral aberrancy. As pure *homo oeconomicus*, we are our financial advisors, investors, and perhaps beneficiaries. We are hedge funds to be managed and maximized.

Here I shall interject yet another parenthesis. The "Birth of Biopolitics" lectures were delivered between 1978 and 1979, following the lectures "Security, Territory, Population" from 1977–78. In the fourth lecture (February 1, 1978) of the "Security, Territory, Population" series Foucault says that these two lecture courses are really a "History of Governmentality."[32] In fact, I have the Suhrkamp two-volume box set in German, which appeared before the English translation, published as *Die Geschichte der Gouvernementalität*.[33] Now, in the 1977–78 lectures Foucault spends a lot of time linking the transformation of pastoral power into biopolitical power. However, both forms of power are modalities of governmentality, which is linked to practices of the self and games of veridiction, new names for genealogies of the self, of knowledge and of power. The analytics of neoliberalism in the second volume is part of the history of governmentality, a new form of governmentality that is meant to conduct subjects by conducting them the least. Neoliberal political rationality can be reduced to the following axiom: The best rule is that which rules the least. Or in the language of Tea Party types and priests of neoliberalism: The best government is the government that governs the least. In the analytics of pastoral power, which incidentally is how Foucault opens his 1979 Tanner Lectures, "Omnes et Singulatim: Towards a Criticism of 'Political Reason,'" there is implicit what he calls the rise of counter-conducts.

I want to argue, therefore, that Foucault, who was particularly sensitive to the "anxiety of influence" (Harold Bloom's apt expression), studiously stayed away from any reference to the "imaginary." The 1960s and 1970s were saturated with Jacques Lacan's and Gaston Bachelard's language of the imaginary. And yet what Foucault called political reason was meant to refer to the whole political imaginary that became hegemonic during the second half of the twentieth century with the emergence of neoliberalism. On the other hand, while Foucault did not explicitly raise the issue of how neoliberalism would instigate its own counter-conducts, at least not in this course of the Tanner lectures, the specter of resistance to neoliberalism had already been raised in the lectures from 1977–78. I contend that this issue returns in the 1979–80 lectures, *On the Government of the Living*, which turn to the Greeks and the early Christians, and their respective practices of confession, which as we know will lead to Foucault's analysis of *parrhesia*, or fearless speech.

This parenthesis is not meant to either invalidate or challenge Brown's criticism of Foucault's limitations in the "formulation of the political," but rather, to raise the question of how Foucault thought that a turn toward practices of *metanoia* and confession was in part a way to begin to decipher how neoliberalism would engender its own counter-conducts. I want to suggest as well that while the lectures on the so-called history of governmentality were meant to cut off the sovereign's head and liberate us from the Hobbesian Leviathan, his analysis of neoliberalism still remains too state-centric. By abandoning the modern period and "returning" to the Greeks, Foucault wanted to think beyond or before the rise of the state, that is, the modern Hobbesian state. I am nonetheless grateful that Brown used the Foucauldian ladder to perform her critique of the hegemony of the political imaginary of neoliberalism and then threw it away. Her distinct analytics of the *femina domestica* is something that is certainly not within the horizon of Foucault's analytics.

4. *FEMINA DOMESTICA* AND NEOLIBERAL GENDER

Wendy Brown has been contributing for over three decades to the feminist project of the critique of Western political philosophy's entrenched and inveterate masculinism, beginning with her 1988 book *Manhood and Politics: A Feminist Reading in Political Theory*[34] and continuing through her most recent work on neoliberalism, as evidenced by *Undoing the Demos* and her opening chapter for this book. In this closing section of my chapter, I focus on what Brown has to say about the deployment of gender and its transformation under neoliberalism's political rationality. Given neoliberalism's logic of turning *homo politicus* into *homo eoconomicus*, with the entailment that all relations, including those of oneself to oneself and of oneself to others, are rendered as economic relations, then an inevitable question would be: What happens to gender under this hypereconomic, that is, hyperindividualistic, regime in which everything is leveled to the lowest denominator of economic transactions? Given that one of neoliberalism's targets is the "social" as such, then it would be easy to assume that neoliberals would also want to dispense with reference to either gender or the dynamics related to gender formations. If we think of gender as fundamentally the ways in which society imprints itself on subjects through its modalities of gender formation—that is, if we think of gender as forms of subject constitution and subjection by social forces and logics—neoliberal rationality would aim to challenge it or critique it. Yet, and as Brown most eloquently demonstrates, this is far from the truth. Gender, it turns out, is indispensable, nay, central to the neoliberal project of economizing all social relations. Part of Brown's genealogical critique of neoliberalism is to unmask the ways in which it ontologizes both the individual and the family. It is this dual ontologization that enables neoliberals to ontologize markets. If neoliberalism, as I noted above, requires the reintroduction of the state of nature back into the civil compact, reversing the Hobbesian logic of our departure from the brutish state of the war of all against all, then Hobbesian atomism and the idea that individuals come embedded within unitary and nuclear families is thus also smuggled back into our social-political imaginary. Brown, light years ahead of Foucault's analysis of the gender dynamics of neoliberalism, unveils the ways in which neoliberal rationality, instead of dispensing with gender as a site of modes of domination and exploitation, is in fact intimately parasitic on its dissimulated use of gender for ever more subtle forms of domination and exploitation. Brown asks, "Does the ascendancy of *homo oeconomicus* and its specific formulation as human capital gender contemporary social arrangements more intensively or differently than its liberal democratic capital predecessors?," to which she answers, "I think that the answer is that gender subordination is both intensified and fundamentally altered."[35] The intensification comes through the neoliberal attack on the "welfare state," through privatization and the shrinking of many social programs aimed at providing a safety net for women, mothers, children, and retirees (who tend to be women given their longevity). Brown lists some of the affected infrastructure, and I quote her list, lest we forget what is being demolished and slashed: "Such infrastructure includes, but is not limited to[,] affordable, quality early childhood and afterschool programs, summer camps, physical and mental healthcare, education, public transportation, neighborhood parks and recreation centers, public pensions, senior centers, and social security."[36] I would add food subsidies for families with incomes under certain levels, as well as access to parenthood advising, support, and clinics where women may receive prenatal and natal care. All of these programs and many others that we took for granted are being rolled back or dismantled under the banner of "responsibilization." Ultimately, individuals and their families are responsible for a whole host of costs that benefit society at large and the market specifically. The neoliberal raison d'état, which says that the best state is the minimal state, translates into a state that detaches itself from any mediation or so-called intervention in the family. To the feminist slogan "The personal is the political," neoliberals respond, "The private is the private, and the political is the economic," or better yet, "It's the economy, stupid."

Brown is quick to point out, however, that the moralizing logic of "responsibilization" turns out to be a means for "penalizing" disproportionally women, who are also disproportionally responsible for those who cannot care for themselves.[37] It is in this way that "familialism"— the postulate that the family is a natural and not a social-political institution—is a constitutive and indispensable aspect of neoliberalism's aim to privatize and de-étaticize the family (by which I mean to dismantle state programs that contribute to the health of the family). I would hazard to extend Brown's claims and add that under neoliberalism, gender exploitation and subordination are exacerbated. The more gender

95

is naturalized and relegated to the private sphere and the family, the more women and their dependents are exploited. Gender relations and gender formations become sites for capitalist extraction, either through direct extraction, as in the exploitation of the affective labor invested by women in their relations as mothers, wives, and caregivers, or indirectly through market labor competition. It is in this sense that we could say that neoliberalism "marketizes" gender, where gender becomes an economic vector of accumulation (for men) and dispossession (for women).

Brown is also keen on elucidating the ways in which gender is transformed by the new neoliberal rationality. This transformation takes the form of the invisibilization of gender relations as the locus of modes of both subordination and exploitation. The more gender is relegated to the family and the private sphere, the more gender disappears from the horizons of the social and the political. Brown uses an interesting formulation to explain the disappearing of gender from our democratic political imaginaries. She writes: "Now divested of a place in language, visually and discursively absent from public consciousness, these forces shaping women's lives are intensified by privatizing formerly public goods and sheering benefits from part-time labor in which women are disproportionally employed."[38] I think this is a powerful formulation, for the abduction of gender from the political and social "lexicon" of democratic struggles has resulted in the overall impoverishment of our political vernaculars. In fact, with the invisibilization and silencing of gender from our democratic political imaginary and vocabularies, we are no longer able to state claims about our social relations and conditions that only three decades ago we were able to do. Brown puts it this way: "While neoliberal *homo oeconomicus* is both gendered and gendering in its ascendancy and dissemination, this is illegible within its own terms."[39]

Neoliberal rationality is also an attack on our political vocabulary, the political vernaculars of democracy, and one of its main victims is gender as a political term. Gender was and remains, for the time being, a *Grundbegriffe* (fundamental concept) and an indispensable term in the lexicon of the struggle for the democratization of the state and of gender relations that are constitutive of the lifeworld. Brown's gendered analysis of neoliberalism—namely, of how neoliberal rationality is "gendered and gendering"—shows what we can call, using the language of Carole Pateman, the new sexual contract or the neoliberal sexual contract.[40] In this new sexual contract, gender is muted and erased, even as gender relations, as relations that mediate the market, the family, and the state, notwithstanding their alleged obsolescence, nonetheless remain indispensable for social wealth extraction and private capital accumulation.

97

I close this gendered critique of neoliberalism with a couple of questions that aim to urge Brown to link her analysis of what she calls "repressive desublimation"[41] and "desublimated freedom" with the overtly anti-feminist and anti-woman tenor of the neoliberal lingo. First, if under neoliberalism gender is privatized, silenced, and erased from our political vocabularies, how is it that many of the authoritarian leaders that have risen from the ashes of neoliberalism are so vocally and loudly anti-woman? As María Pía Lara has noted in a recent essay for the *Los Angeles Review of Books*, the ascendancy of global authoritarian regimes has come in lockstep with the ascendancy of a backlash against feminists in particular and women in general.[42] This is captured in Trump's "nasty woman" invective against Hillary Clinton but is amply demonstrated by the vitriolic, crude, and violence-inciting language of most of these authoritarian movements. How are we to explain this dual erasure of gender from our political lexicon and its seemingly concomitant weaponization of a certain kind of wounded and aggrieved masculinity? In an essay from May 22, 2018, titled "What Was Emancipation?," Brown writes, powerfully, the following: "Freedom as a right of aggression against social mores, protections, and justice; freedom as entitlement to refuse democratic principles and accountability; freedom as anti-social and antipolitical, and freedom that is perfectly compatible with undemocratic governments—this is what neoliberalism bore to the world. And, when this formation is also energized by the rancor of wounded whiteness—wounds generated by neoliberal *economic* effects—it can become freedom with a fascist glint in its eye."[43] I entirely agree. I would add, however, that this antisocial and antipolitical freedom is also an authoritarian freedom that is a misogynist freedom, a freedom that declares itself free of any social strictures, any rules of civility, and that is shamelessly "pussy grabbing." How are we to explain the desublimation of male freedom to both factually and symbolically perform violence against women, when the very language of gender is made unintelligible by the forces of neoliberalism?

My second question has to do with the inchoate counter-conducts that every exercise of power instigates. Not to sound Pollyannaish, but in the shadow of neoliberalism, with its exacerbation of gender exploitation, new forms of thinking gender have emerged. There is now a plethora of gender specifications: gay, lesbian, polyamorous, bisexual, nonbinary, transgender, and so on. One may speak of the liberation of gender from sex, as if under neoliberalism we learned to think that gender is a private matter but that it goes all the way down. On the one hand, gender is naturalized within the family, as we noted above, but on the other hand, gender is made fluid, nonnatural or naturalizable. Under neoliberalism, this means there are more modalities, more ways, in which gender is lived and thus many more ways in which it may be turned into human capital. If capitalist commodification turned discontent and dissent into commodities, neoliberalism turns gender into a market asset. Gender fluidity may be the means for the marketization of gender, but it may also be the means through which forms of resistance are enacted. At the very least, the #MeToo movement and the gender fluidity movements of the millennials have decoupled gender from the binary logic of sex, and in this way they have enriched and potentially transformed the vocabularies of feminism.

NOTES

1. Henry Louis Gates Jr., *Stony the Road: Reconstruction, White Supremacy, and the Rise of Jim Crow* (New York: Penguin, 2019).
2. Ta-Nehisi Coates, *We Were Eight Years in Power: An American Tragedy* (New York: One World, 2017).
3. Ibid., 344.
4. Eric Foner, *Reconstruction: America's Unfinished Revolution, 1863–1967*, updated ed. (New York: Harper Perennial, 2002).
5. Wendy Brown, *Politics Out of History* (Princeton: Princeton University Press, 2001), 93.
6. Ibid.
7. Friedrich Nietzsche, *On the Genealogy of Morality*, trans. Carol Diethe (Cambridge: Cambridge University Press, 2007).
8. Nietzsche quoted by Brown, in *Politics Out of History*, 97.

9. Here what Foucault has to say about history in *Society Must Be Defended* is especially relevant. See Michel Foucault, *"Society Must Be Defended": Lectures at the Collège de France, 1975–1976*, trans. David Macey (New York: Picador, 2003), in particular, lecture 3 from January 21, 1976.

10. Brown, *Politics Out of History*, 104; emphasis added.

11. Michel Foucault, "Nietzsche, Genealogy, History," quoted by Brown, in ibid., 106.

12. See Friedrich Nietzsche, *On the Advantage and Disadvantage of History for Life*, trans., with an introduction, by Peter Preuss (Indianapolis, IN: Hackett, 1980).

13. Michel Foucault, "The Art of Telling the Truth," quoted by Brown in *Politics Out of History*, 107.

14. Take, for instance, this statement by Foucault: "Three domains of genealogy are possible. First, an historical ontology of ourselves in relation to truth through which we constitute ourselves as subjects of knowledge; second, an historical ontology of ourselves in relation to a field of power through which we constitute ourselves as subjects acting on others; third, an historical ontology in relation to ethics through which we constitute ourselves as moral agents." In Hubert L. Dreyfus and Paul Rabinow, *Michel Foucault: Beyond Structuralism and Hermeneutics*, 2nd ed. (Chicago: University of Chicago Press, 1983), 237.

15. See ibid.

16. Brown, *Politics Out of History*, 109.

17. Georg Wilhelm Friedrich Hegel, *Elements of the Philosophy of Right*, trans. H. B. Nisbet (Cambridge: Cambridge University Press, 1991), 21; emphasis in original.

18. Brown, *Politics Out of History*, 109.

19. Ibid., 112.

20. Ibid., 113; italics in original.

21. Bernard-Henri Lévy, *Adventures on the Freedom Road: The French Intellectuals in the 20th Century* (London: Harvill Press, 1995), 371.

22. Brown, *Politics Out of History*, 94.

23. See, in particular, ibid., 119.

24. Wendy Brown, *Undoing the Demos: Neoliberalism's Stealth Revolution* (New York: Zone Books, 2015).

25. See Naomi Klein, *The Shock Doctrine: The Rise of Disaster Capitalism* (New York: Picador, 2007).

26. Brown, *Undoing the Demos*, 30.

27. Ibid., 62–69.

28. Ibid., 73.

29. Ibid.

30. Ibid., 74.

31. Ibid.

32. See Thomas Lemke, *Foucault's Analysis of Modern Governmentality: A Critique of Political Reason*, trans. Erik Butler (London: Verso, 2019), especially the "Preface to the English-Language Edition."

33. Michel Foucault, *Die Geschichte der Gouvernementalität*, trans. Claudia Brede-Konersmann and Jürgen Schröder, 2 vols. (Frankfurt am Main: Suhrkamp Verlag, 2006).

34. Wendy Brown, *Manhood and Politics: A Feminist Reading in Political Theory* (Totowa, NJ: Rowman & Littlefield, 1988).
35. Brown, *Undoing the Demos*, 105.
36. Ibid.
37. Ibid.
38. Ibid., 106.
39. Ibid.
40. See Carole Pateman, *The Sexual Contract* (Stanford: Stanford University Press, 1988).
41. See Wendy Brown, "Neoliberalism's Frankenstein: Authoritarian Freedom in Twenty-First Century 'Democracies,'" in Wendy Brown, Peter E. Gordon, and Max Pensky, *Authoritarianism: Three Inquiries in Critical Theory* (Chicago: University of Chicago Press, 2018), 29–36; and Brown, *In the Ruins of Neoliberalism: The Rise of Antidemocratic Politics in the West* (New York: Columbia University Press, 2019), 163–68.
42. María Pía Lara, "Habermas's Concept of the Public Sphere and the New Feminist Agenda," *Los Angeles Review of Books*, July 31, 2019.
43. Wendy Brown, "What Was Emancipation?," MS (May 22, 2018), 2. I want to thank Prof. Brown for sharing this manuscript with me.

CHAPTER 6

Feminism Against Neoliberalism

Questioning the Political with Wendy Brown

Johanna Oksala

An important theme in Wendy Brown's work has been the hidden under-belly of politics, the constitutive outside that has been suppressed, disavowed, and excluded from the sphere recognized as the political. In her masterful readings of political philosophy, Brown not only shows how Western thought and understanding of politics are built on the "tacit presumption of the relative boundedness and autonomy of the political," but how, on closer scrutiny, such a presumption must be exposed as an illusion.[1] While politics is traditionally understood to be distinct from domains such as the economic, the social, the cultural, the natural, or the private, Brown shows that questions about the nature of the political cannot presume such autonomy.

The autonomy of the political is compromised not just because the excluded outside becomes constitutive of the inside in a conceptual sense. The claim is stronger: the outside is constitutive of the inside in a very concrete and material sense. In her first book, *Manhood and Politics*, Brown presents insightful and provocative interpretations of Aristotle, Machiavelli, and Weber, showing how each of these authors' masculine conception of politics presumes an excluded feminine outside. The political activities of creating history and meaning are ideologically and practically divided off from the feminine outside containing the indispensable activities of maintaining and sustaining life.[2] The autonomy of the political can therefore never be complete. Attempts to overcome nature and necessity can only result in politics that is "extremely fragile, restless, and anxious about its power and autonomy."[3] Since politics is fundamentally dependent on its outside, it is easily threatened or contaminated by the excluded inferior elements supporting it and giving it life.[4]

In Brown's later work, the argument becomes historically more specific by homing in on liberalism in particular, revealing its constitutive outside and outsiders.[5] The key argument is structurally similar: the supporting elements of liberalism are fundamentally gendered and feminized but also importantly depoliticized, both ideologically and practically. Brown shows how the subject of liberalism as a figure of self-interest and self-orientation is at odds with what women have been constituted as. The autonomous woman—the childless, unmarried, or lesbian woman—has been the sign of a disorderly society or of an individual failure to "adapt to femininity." For Brown, such "unnatural" figures expose how the social order presumed by liberalism is itself pervasively gendered, representing both a gendered division of labor and a gendered division of the sensibilities and activities of subjects. Women's traditional role in the family has been to surrender their self-interest so that their husbands and children can attain their autonomous subjectivity. The constitutive terms of liberal political discourse and practice—individual, autonomy, self-interest—thus fundamentally depend upon their implicit opposition to a subject and a set of activities marked as "feminine," while effectively obscuring this dependence.[6]

The important upshot of Brown's project of exposing the constitutive and gendered underside of politics is that we need "a formulation of the political that is richer, more complicated, and also perhaps more fragile than that circumscribed by institutions, procedures, and political representation."[7] The political must be recognized as "a terrain of struggle without fixed or metaphysical referents and a terrain of power's irreducible and pervasive presence in human affairs."[8] This insight is, in my view, of particular importance for feminist theory. As feminist theorists have insisted, such an open-ended understanding of the political implies that we can potentially find politics everywhere—"in cultural, familial, economic, and psychosexual relations, and more."[9] In short, the personal is political, but so are the natural, the economic, and the social.

However, at times, Brown falls back on a more traditional conception of the political—a conception that attributes fixed metaphysical or at least transhistorical content to it. While she recognizes the importance of "politicization"—the attempt to reveal relations of power in something ordinarily conceived of in other terms—she nevertheless insists that the political must retain its distinctiveness. "The theoretical politicization of any activity or relations is not the same as theorizing the political."[10] The political must remain "the distinct problematic of the values and powers binding collectivities."[11]

The efforts in political thought to define what these values and powers are have repeatedly run into difficulties, however. Whether we think of Carl Schmitt's definition of the political as always referring to the friend/enemy distinction, or of Hannah Arendt's contested distinction between the social and the political, the problem with defining the political as a distinct and autonomous domain is that certain questions, issues, and experiences are thus placed outside of politics.[12] To put the problem in more provocative terms, purely ontological investigation into the nature of the political turns out to be a political act itself, establishing the boundaries of the realm of "genuine politics."

My concern is that the tension between these two contrasting views of the political in Brown's thought—the political understood either as a distinct and substantive sphere in its own right or as the result of historically contingent struggles of politicization—produces some problematic consequences for her analysis of neoliberal governmentality, and particularly for the contemporary feminist critiques of neoliberalism. I am ready to concede that the consistency of a thinker's position might be an overrated virtue in political theory and that theoretical questions about the political often risk becoming armchair philosophizing par excellence. But I hope to show that questioning the political has important consequences for our contemporary critiques of neoliberalism, as well as for our politics against it.

103

The discussion proceeds in two parts. In the first section I focus mainly on Brown's critique of neoliberalism in *Undoing the Demos*. I pose questions to Brown regarding the figure of *homo politicus* central to her argument, as well as questioning the distinction between the economic and the political spheres underlying her critique. In the second section, I show how the tension between the two different conceptions of the political is connected to the strains in Brown's analyses of the contemporary gendering of the political realm. I conclude by defending the importance of Marxist-feminist analyses of social reproduction for an adequate theoretical and political response to the current challenges that feminist politics faces against neoliberalism.

1. THE POLITICAL AND THE ECONOMIC

In *Undoing the Demos*, Brown presents a powerful critique of neoliberalism and its devastating effects on democracy. The critique builds mainly on Foucault's lectures *The Birth of Biopolitics*, but Brown also devotes substantial sections of the book to a critique of Foucault, attempting to show how his account of neoliberalism is both outdated and flawed in significant respects.[13]

A key issue in Brown's criticism of Foucault is his conception of the political, which she equates with government. Brown claims Foucault's conception of the political is "largely limited to the (ironically, state-centered) terms of 'sovereignty' and 'juridicism.'"[14] This allegedly limited conception of the political domain underlying Foucault's analysis is "inadequate for capturing what neoliberalism has done to social life, culture, subjectivity, and, above all, politics."[15] Moreover, it is fatal for our attempts to develop effective resistances against it, because "there is no *political* body, no demos acting in concert (even episodically) or expressing aspirational sovereignty; there are few social forces from below and no shared powers of rule or shared struggles for freedom."[16] Brown contends that while "these absences are a perennial limitation of Foucault's work for political theory," they are especially significant for our contemporary critiques of neoliberalism.[17]

Brown proposes a revision of Foucault's account that makes central a figuration of the subject that Foucault completely ignored—namely, *homo politicus*. According to Brown, *homo politicus* is clearly distinct from the economic subject, *homo oeconomicus*, as well as from the subject of rights, *homo legalis*. Foucault's mistake was to omit this important figuration of the human from his account of modern thought and practice, with the consequence that he failed to fully understand what was at stake in the ascendency of neoliberalism and what the prospects were for contesting its table of values.[18]

Brown sketches a brief history of *homo politicus* from Aristotle to Rousseau and Mill in order to show that the prominence of man's economic features in modern thought and practice never before fully extinguished his political features. She defines *homo politicus* with such distinctly human capacities as "moral reflection, deliberation, and expression."[19] *Homo politicus* is "a language-using, moral, and associational creature who utilizes these capacities to govern himself with others."[20] Her contention is that even when these capacities became suffused with the project of serving God in the centuries between antiquity and modernity, man nevertheless continued to be defined by them.[21] "*Homo oeconomicus* certainly ascends and expands its dominion in Euro-Atlantic modernity, but *homo politicus* remains alive and important through this time, as well—full of demands and expectations, the seat of political sovereignty, freedom and legitimacy."[22] The neoliberal insistence that there are only rational market actors in every sphere of life, is, according to Brown, "novel, indeed, revolutionary, in the history of the West."[23]

Brown's key contention is that, in its democratic form, *homo politicus* could be the chief weapon against neoliberal reason's instantiation as a governing rationality, "the resource for opposing it with another set of claims and another vision of existence."[24] In other words, Brown argues that if we could resuscitate this political subject, it could form "the substance and legitimacy of whatever democracy might mean," as well as provide a grounding for such values as "political equality and freedom, representation, popular sovereignty, and deliberation and judgement about the public good and the common."[25] She formulates the stakes in stark terms: if *homo oeconomicus* succeeds in completely vanquishing *homo politicus*, "this would darken the globe against all possibilities of democratic or other just futures."[26]

My questions to Brown are: Do we really need to rescue this humanist figuration of the political subject for our contemporary critiques of neoliberalism? And perhaps more important, even if we wanted to rescue it, *can* we do it? How can we ground our critiques of neoliberalism on such a figure in our postfoundational and post-humanist theoretical landscape, in which political critiques built on essentialist notions of human beings have been discarded to the dust heap of reactionary and outdated theory? Do we not, rather, need to invent new figurations of the subject, new forms of subjectivities, and new political idioms? Or to formulate these questions in the framework of governmentality, what kind of governmentality does *homo politicus* correspond with? If the key problem of neoliberalism, according to both Brown and Foucault, is that the democratic liberal state is remade from one founded in juridical sovereignty to one modeled on a business, and correspondingly, juridical subjects are reconstrued as economic subjects, where does the figure of *homo politicus* fit into this transformation? And finally, as feminists, do we not need to be troubled about the fact that the *homo politicus* that persisted through modernity was not only moral and associational, but also male, white, and owned property?

My concern is that Brown's analysis of the opposing figures of *homo oeconomicus* and *homo politicus* ultimately builds on, reiterates, and entrenches a transhistorical distinction between two distinct spheres, "the economic" and "the political," with different objectives, procedures, and instruments. Her critique of Foucault and his omission of *homo politicus* is thus grounded on a distinctly different understanding of the political than the one developed by Foucault. Brown builds her critique of neoliberalism on a tacit assumption of a relatively fixed separation between the political and the economic spheres, a separation that neoliberalism now has the unprecedented power of eroding in favor of the economic. Brown's key problem regarding neoliberalism is thus repeatedly formulated as "the neoliberal economization of the political."[27] But how, exactly, should we understand the ontological status of these two separate domains—the economic and the political—and what does the neoliberal economization of the political sphere mean? Brown makes clear that by economization, she does not mean literal marketization. "To speak of the relentless and ubiquitous economization of all features of life by neoliberalism is . . . not to claim that neoliberalism literally *marketizes* all spheres, even as such marketization is certainly one important effect of neoliberalism."[28] Rather, economization should be understood as metaphorical in the sense that *the model of the market* is disseminated to all domains and activities.[29] In other words, social interactions are made intelligible through market evaluations, even when they do not necessarily involve actually handing over money for goods. One might approach one's dating life, for example, in the mode of an entrepreneur or an investor.[30] Neoliberal economization means that market principles come to frame every sphere and activity, "from mothering to mating, from learning to criminality, from planning ones' family to planning one's death."[31] They also come to reframe and even replace democratic institutions and a democratic public, as well as "all that such a public represents at its best."[32]

Brown's claim about the economization of the political is thus a philosophical or an ontological claim about the way we have come to conceptually frame, rationalize, and understand ourselves and our world, not a literal or empirical claim about actual markets. However, depending on our understanding of the political, there are still at least two ways of interpreting this idea.

The first one is that there is a substantive and normative content to the political, providing it with distinctiveness and autonomy, that is now compromised or encroached upon by something fundamentally foreign to it. Brown never formulates this content definitively but refers to Aristotle, Arendt, and Marx and appropriates their ontological distinction between the economic and the political as denoting the spheres of necessity, mere life, and survival, on the one hand, and ethical and political freedom, on the other. "As economic parameters become the only parameters for all conduct and concern, the limited form of human existence that Aristotle and Hannah Arendt designated as 'mere life' and that Marx called life 'confined by necessity' . . . this limited form and imaginary becomes ubiquitous and total *across* classes. Neoliberal rationality eliminates what these thinkers termed 'good life' (Aristotle), or 'the true realm of freedom' (Marx), by which they did not mean luxury, leisure, or indulgence, but rather the cultivation and expression of distinctly human capacities for ethical and political freedom, creativity, unbounded reflection, or invention."[33] In paragraphs such as this, Brown grounds her critique of neoliberalism on a substantive and transhistorical conception of the political defined as "good life" and "the true realm of freedom."[34] Neoliberalism must be resisted because it is corrupting this genuine or original form of politics and transforming it into a perverted and corrupted form emptied of substance and "intellectual seriousness."[35] In other words, until fairly recently, the political had a distinct nature and meaning. Neoliberalism now has the unprecedented power of erasing them.[36]

Against such a normative and transhistorical understanding of the political, the other alternative is to follow Foucault and to insist that the domain of the political is thoroughly historical and constructed in shifting practices of power. What we understand as the political today is the result of historically contingent struggles of politicization, struggles that have been, to a large extent, buried and forgotten, resulting in seemingly fixed, "naturalized" or transhistorical conceptions of the political. Because power relations are rooted in the whole network of society, political analysis cannot be reduced to the study of a series of institutions that would merit the name "political."[37] The political must, rather, be understood as a historically variable zone of rationalization and division of power that is coextensive with society.[38]

As Brown writes, we learned from Foucault that "the economy" is not a transhistorical category. Rather, the way the economy is conceived and positioned in relation to other spheres of life, other systems of meaning, and other fields of activity is always historically shifting.[39] Foucault's lectures on liberal governmentality, *Security, Territory, Population*, provide us with a genealogy of the economic—not a history of the concept but a history of the governmentality that established the economic sphere as an autonomous realm of reality with its own laws and regularities. For Foucault, physiocrats such as François Quesnay and their economic doctrine represent "the founding act of economic thought," in the sense that with them not only a whole new conception of the economy emerges but, crucially, the free market starts to operate as the principle of good government.[40] Foucault's key argument in these lectures is that it would be wrong to simply concede that physiocratic economic theory produced a shift in economic policy as its practical consequence.[41] What occurred instead was a fundamental reorganization of the theoretical field of economics as well as of the techniques of government. Physiocrats rejected any analysis of economic processes in terms of morality and approached them instead as autonomous, natural phenomena governed by scientific laws and regularities. Through the work of the physiocrats a modern conception of the economy emerged as an autonomous sphere of society and an object of scientific knowledge in political history. This was highly significant for our conception of good government and, more generally, for our understanding of the political. The establishment of an autonomous and self-regulating economic sphere was not a deliberate political act tactically invoked or initiated by anybody, but this does not mean that it had no political effects. A key aim of Foucault's historical ontology is precisely an analysis of these effects on our social reality and our understanding of politics.

Once we recognize the historicity of "the economic" and its constitutive opposition to other spheres of activity, this implies that "the political" cannot be treated as a transhistorical category either. The political gains its meaning from what is historically included in it but also, importantly, from what is excluded through acts of "depoliticization"—acts that demote some practices and power relations to the categories of the economy, nature, necessity, and so on. Resisting "the economization of the political" by neoliberalism would then not consist in a nostalgic attempt to protect the illusory autonomy of the political but rather in questioning all transhistorical meanings of it. We have to ask how the boundaries between such supposedly fixed ontological categories as "the political" and "the economic" are drawn in actual practices of power in particular historical circumstances and what political functions such boundaries serve in neoliberal capitalism. A central idea in many contemporary critiques of neoliberalism, including Brown's, is that the neoliberal rendering of policy issues as economic rather than as social, cultural, or political crucially signifies that they are understood as morally and politically neutral and can therefore be removed from democratic decision-making processes to the exclusive territory of economic experts and financial institutions. The incongruous question that the Left, in its attempts to thwart the advancements of neoliberalism, has repeatedly had to face is, How can we resist politically economic truths, which are supposed to be politically neutral?

To sum up this section, when we view neoliberalism not just as an economic policy but as a political rationality embedded in diffuse practices, then resistance against it must bring together many kinds of seemingly separate struggles—struggles for democracy, but also feminist struggles and ecological struggles, as well as struggles for racial and sexual justice, for example. These diverse struggles must draw their political strength from different, and sometimes even conflicting, noneconomic normativities. Such a wide coalition of resistances requires practicing solidarity as an active principle, but it also requires an open-ended understanding of the political. We cannot assume that there is a fixed, normative, and transhistorical content to the political providing it with distinctiveness and autonomy that is now compromised or encroached upon by something that is fundamentally foreign to it. Rather, resisting neoliberalism requires, most fundamentally, the broad politicization of the meanings it constitutes and the practices it installs.

2. FEMINIST POLITICS AGAINST NEOLIBERALISM

For feminist theory and politics, the problems arising from a fixed and transhistorical conception of the political, such as that found in the thought of Aristotle and Arendt, are particularly pronounced. "Genuine politics" becomes divorced from the historical activities related to the production and maintenance of life, from questions of economic and social justice, as well as from personal and intimate power relations. As Brown's own masterful readings of Aristotle and Arendt show, these thinkers asserted the value and autonomy of politics as a unique and ennobling dimension of human existence, but at the expense of life, bodily desires, and demands.[42]

Feminists must be able to pose critical questions, not only about the viability of democratic institutions and procedures but also about the potential threats neoliberal governmentality poses to those values and practices, which were never admitted to the realm of the political in the first place. As the contentious feminist issue of commercial gestational surrogacy, for example, makes clear, a key political question today is whether different processes of biological life or "nature" are brought within the domain of the markets or whether their appropriate place is considered to be outside of that domain. This has direct consequences for pressing political questions concerning equal access and democratic political control over such processes, but it is also fundamental for the assignment of their meaning and value. Feminists have to ask what happens to women's personhood if the buying and selling of their sexual and reproductive activities, for example, is normalized and becomes widespread. This requires politicizing our conception not just of the economic but also of the natural, the private, the biological.

In *Undoing the Demos*, Brown questions briefly the contemporary gendering of the political realm. She poses the question of what kind of gender order is produced and reproduced when neoliberal political rationality prevails, but she limits her inquiry there largely to the empirical question of what the impact of neoliberalism has been on "those positioned as women in the sexual division of labor that neoliberal orders continue to depend on and reproduce."[43] "When the[se] public provisions are eliminated or privatized, the work and/or the cost of providing them is returned to individuals, disproportionately to women. . . . 'Responsibilization' in the context of privatizing public goods uniquely penalizes women to the extent that they remain disproportionately responsible for those who cannot be responsible for themselves. In this respect, familialism is an essential requirement, rather than an incidental feature of the neoliberal privatization of public goods and services."[44]

Brown's argument reiterates the socialist-feminist critiques of neoliberalism that have sought to demonstrate that its advancement has taken place largely at the expense of women. Feminist critics have argued that not only are women's jobs most affected by cutbacks in public expenditure, as they work more often in the public sector, but that the lack of social services and benefits also further affects women more than men, since they are more dependent on those services.[45] A similar tension between the individual and the family that characterized liberalism now characterizes neoliberalism: there must be other subjects besides *homo oeconomicus* who bind the familial and social order and provision the needs that this neoliberal figuration of the human disavows. "Only performatively male members of a gendered sexual division of labor can even pretend to the kind of autonomy this subject requires."[46]

But doesn't the figuration of the subject, *homo politicus*, which Brown advocates as a resource for opposing neoliberal governmentality, also fundamentally depend on these "invisible practices and unnamed others"?[47] Isn't the distinction between the political and the economic realms that underlies Brown's analysis of the opposing figures of *homo oeconomicus* and *homo politicus* subtended by another figure or figures who are excluded from both of these realms, unnamed and disavowed—namely, the feminine, familial subjects?[48] What would it mean politically to make these "others" and the support they provide fully visible?

In *Edgework*, published in 2005, Brown provides a strikingly different answer to the questions surrounding the gendering of our current political realm, perhaps more consistent with the idea of a gender-neutral *homo politicus*. In a central passage, she writes:

> It is clear enough that women and men can be rendered interchangeable cogs in a contemporary and future capitalist machinery, where physical strength is rarely an issue, where continuity on the job matters little, where reproductive work has been almost completely commodified and reproduction itself is nearly separable from sexed bodies and is in any event separable from a sexual division of labor. Notwithstanding the protracted Marxist-feminist analyses of the indispensability of unpaid housework to the production of surplus value, the home as a necessary if stricken haven in a heartless world, and the need for a malleable surplus army of labor (all of which were straining to prove both the materiality of gender subordination and its necessity to

capitalism), it is evident today that the equal participation and remuneration of women in the economic and civic order can be achieved, even if unevenly and with difficulty.[49]

According to Brown, Marxist-feminism thus came to a dead end because "the feminist ambition to eliminate gender as a site of subordination could technically be met within a capitalist life-form—that is, there is nothing in sexed bodies or even in gender subordination that capitalism cannot live without."[50] But is it really evident that the equal participation and remuneration of women can be achieved in contemporary capitalism? To pose the question in traditional Marxist-feminist terms, does capitalism, and liberalism as its moral justification and political legitimization, structurally require gender subordination, or can the forms of oppression and discrimination based on gender really be eliminated in some current or future form of capitalism such as neoliberal biocapitalism? Or, to formulate the question as a philosophical question about our current conception of the political, can the constitutive outside of the political sphere finally be ungendered, severed from its deep historical and material connection to femininity?

My contention is that in order to even tentatively answer these questions, we need "the protracted Marxist-feminist analyses" of social reproduction.[51] I acknowledge that while these analyses have primarily attempted to make visible the indispensability of unpaid reproductive labor in capitalist society, a countervailing trend has in fact characterized the advancement of neoliberal capitalism in recent decades: we have witnessed an enormous push for the marketization of reproductive work—care work, domestic labor, and even generational reproduction through the commercialization of gestational surrogacy, for example. However, my contention is that there still appear to be some important structural obstacles to the attempts to turn women into *femina economica* and that it is important for feminist theory to acknowledge and investigate them.

Marxist-feminist theorists have forcefully argued that competitive labor markets discriminate against those whose reproductive biology makes them primarily responsible for childbearing.[52] The argument, in a nutshell, is that capitalism, at least in its current forms, structurally depends on biological reproductive processes—pregnancy, childbirth, lactation—to secure the reproduction of the labor force. In an economic system based on wage labor, in which resources are primarily distributed to individuals according to their ability to compete for them, as opposed to their need or their right to these resources, the people who carry the burden of generational reproduction cannot participate in this game on equal terms. Instead, capitalism structurally exploits and economically disadvantages them by placing them in a contradictory position, in which they are expected to both compete in labor markets for the economic resources necessary for survival while, at the same time, also carrying the extra burden of generational reproduction outside of markets.

It is important to acknowledge that Marxist-feminists such as Lise Vogel, for example, who puts forward this argument, do not hold that women's distinctive role in generational reproduction would imply that their oppression was an ahistorical or transhistorical phenomenon determined by their biology. Vogel identifies a biological difference grounding the gendered division of labor in capitalism, but she makes clear that it is not biology per se that dictates women's oppression. The fact that different people are differently involved in the generational reproduction of labor power during pregnancy and lactation is not sufficient by itself to constitute a source of oppression. All kinds of divisions of labor have always existed in societies and do not by themselves determine social hierarchies. Rather, the problem is that in capitalist societies, which are based almost exclusively on wage labor, childbearing capacity creates a significant hindrance to the appropriation of surplus value. As Vogel puts it: "Child-bearing threatens to diminish the contribution a woman can make as a direct producer and as a participant in necessary labor. Pregnancy and lactation involve, at the minimum, several months of somewhat reduced capacity to work."[53]

Vogel contends that the historically specific family forms and gender orders that preexisted capitalism were adopted and reinforced in order to deal with capitalism's contradictory need both to exploit and to renew labor power. As Sheila Rowbotham writes in her now classic study, it is "both immediately more profitable and more politically convenient to utilize the accepted idea that women maintain the family outside the cash-nexus or at least at the lowest conceivable rate granted by the family allowance or social security."[54] Hence, while Marxist-feminists such as Vogel and Rowbotham advance a structural or theoretical argument, it is not a deterministic argument in the sense that capitalism would have deliberately created the heterosexual nuclear family in order to regulate social reproduction or that the patriarchal gender order would form the only imaginable option for reproducing the labor force. However, as long as the fact remains that only some people's bodies have to go through the extra burden of pregnancy and childbirth—and currently the overwhelming majority of them are bodies marked as female—these people have to take at least some time off from paid employment in order to do this.[55]

115

Capitalist societies can, and in some parts of the world are made to, compensate these women for their reproductive labor with various political and social measures external to the market; but at least with our current level of biotechnology, they cannot completely remove this handicap. At worst, these compensatory measures constitute a discriminatory mechanism that legitimizes childbearing women's exclusion from the supposedly free labor markets. While obviously not all women bear children, statistical discrimination against even those women who prioritize their careers means that it is more difficult for them, too, to get hired and promoted.[56]

We can obviously engage in thought experiments on how to level the playing field without abolishing capitalism. The development of artificial wombs or other biotechnological means of producing babies outside of the human body would be one solution. The other possibility would be the eventual dissolution of our current gender and family order to the point of completely uncoupling childbearing from the gender binary.[57] We would then not be discriminating against childbearing women—we would be discriminating against childbearing women, men, and nonbinary people. Finally, the technologically easiest solution, at least in the short term, would be to completely commodify gestation and open up literal markets for children.

My aim here is not to try to advocate any of these possibilities. Rather, it is merely to question the idea that "there is nothing in sexed bodies or even in gender subordination that capitalism cannot live without."[58] When we foreground social reproduction, particularly generational reproduction, in our assessments of neoliberal capitalism, the connection between capitalism and gender oppression appears less like a contingent historical configuration that could be dissolved with relative ease and more like a structural necessity. Hence, when Brown notes that in contemporary capitalism "reproduction itself is nearly separable from sexed bodies," I want to insist that we have to continue to emphasize the word "nearly."[59]

The gender order that neoliberalism produces is deeply conflicted, unequal, and divisive, but the idea that neoliberalism would spell the end of Marxist-feminism is, in my view, false. On the contrary, my contention is neoliberalism is giving left feminist struggles against capitalism a renewed force and urgency.[60] The same neoliberal forces that have pushed some professional women into the position of mistresses while others have become maids also heighten the political importance of social reproduction, not just for neoliberal capitalism but also for our struggles against it. Rather than resisting neoliberalism through recourse to the traditional humanist figure of *homo politicus*, I want to suggest that feminist politics centering on social reproduction could provide us with alternative models for collectively confronting neoliberal capitalism.

The details of what such feminist politics might look like are unfortunately beyond the scope of this chapter. Zhivka Valiavicharska suggests that such feminist politics might mean direct actions, occupations, blockades, and militant marches but also, and importantly, "care work, material support, jail support, the work of healing—work which remains invisible and does not register politically, but nevertheless reproduces and sustains our struggles, as well as giving communities in struggle the strength and resilience to carry on in the long run."[61] Wanda Vrasti places second-wave feminism, and its refusal to separate the political and the personal, in the lineage of New Left politics and tactics stretching from the late 1960s all the way to the recent Occupy and Indignados movements. The domestic sphere is not important for feminists because it is the sphere of "women's work" but because it constitutes a dimension of collective living otherwise banished from life under capitalism.[62]

116

I want to make clear, however, that whatever concrete form such politics takes, it cannot take the form of identity politics—an exclusive project built on fixed identity and including only childbearing "natural women." On the contrary, I think that the Marxist-feminist position that foregrounds the importance of social reproduction for capitalism clearly shows that the social organization of reproductive labor is an issue that cannot be limited to the specific interests of any particular group.[63] Rather, it has to be understood as a political issue that directly concerns the future and economic productivity of society as a whole. Although the liberal political framework effectively portrays generational reproduction as a consumer choice—the decision to have a child is another costly preference—from a Marxist-feminist perspective children have to be recognized as a necessary condition for any form of continuing social life as well as economic production. Feminist politics must acknowledge this and pose questions about our collective responsibility for it and its consequences for all of us, irrespective of our gender. The militant queer-feminist politics against neoliberalism that I am envisaging would thus also have to confront the male-dominated Left, as well as the male-centric histories that define our understanding of politics and political subjects.

NOTES

1. Wendy Brown, *Edgework: Critical Essays on Knowledge and Politics* (Princeton: Princeton University Press, 2005), 61.
2. Wendy Brown, *Manhood and Politics: A Feminist Reading in Political Theory* (Totowa, NJ: Rowman & Littlefield, 1988), 192.
3. Ibid., 43.
4. Ibid.
5. See, e.g., Brown, *States of Injury: Power and Freedom in Late Modernity* (Princeton: Princeton University Press, 1995); and Brown, *Edgework*.
6. Brown, *States of Injury*, 152.
7. Ibid., 9.
8. Ibid., 37.
9. Wendy Brown, *Edgework*, 75.
10. Ibid., 76.
11. Ibid.

12. See, for example, Carl Schmitt, *The Concept of the Political* (Chicago: University of Chicago Press, 1996); Hannah Arendt, *On Revolution* (London: Penguin, 1990); Hannah Arendt, *The Human Condition* (Chicago: University of Chicago Press, 1998).

13. See Michel Foucault, *The Birth of Biopolitics: Lectures at the Collège de France 1978–1979*, ed. Michel Senellart (Basingstoke, UK: Palgrave Macmillan, 2008).

14. Wendy Brown, *Undoing the Demos: Neoliberalism's Stealth Revolution* (New York: Zone Books, 2015), 73.

15. Brown, *Undoing the Demos*, 73.

16. Ibid.

17. Ibid., 74.

18. Ibid., 86.

19. Ibid., 88.

20. Ibid., 91.

21. Ibid.

22. Ibid., 98.

23. Ibid., 99.

24. Ibid., 87.

25. Ibid.

26. Ibid.

27. See, e.g., ibid., 17, 109, 208.

28. Ibid., 31.

29. Ibid.

30. Ibid.

31. Ibid., 67.

32. Ibid., 39.

33. Ibid., 43.

34. Ibid.

35. Ibid., 39.

36. Ibid., 122.

37. Michel Foucault, "The Subject and Power," in *Michel Foucault: Beyond Structuralism and Hermeneutics*, ed. Hubert Dreyfus and Paul Rabinow (Chicago: University of Chicago Press, 1982), 224.

38. Michel Foucault, *Power/Knowledge: Selected Interviews and Other Writings 1972–1977*, ed. Colin Gordon (Brighton, UK: Harvester, 1980), 189.

39. Brown, *Undoing the Demos*, 81, 83. Brown also refers to Timothy Mitchell, who writes that "the economy," a noun with a definite article naming an objective domain, came into being only in the 1940s and 1950s. See Brown, *Undoing the Demos*, 81; and Timothy Mitchell, *Rule of Experts: Egypt, Techno-Politics, Modernity* (Berkeley: University of California Press, 2002), 3–7.

40. Michel Foucault, *Security, Territory, Population: Lectures at the Collège de France 1977–78*, ed. Michel Senellart (Basingstoke, UK: Palgrave Macmillan, 2007), 33.

41. Foucault, *Security, Territory, Population*, 36.

42. See Brown, *Manhood and Politics*.

43. Brown, *Undoing the Demos*, 107.

44. Ibid., 105–6.

118

45. See, e.g., Hester Eisenstein, *Feminism Seduced: How Global Elites Use Women's Labor and Ideas to Exploit the World* (Boulder, CO: Paradigm, 2009); Sylvia Walby, *The Future of Feminism* (Cambridge, UK: Polity Press, 2011).

46. Brown, *Undoing the Demos*, 103.

47. Ibid.

48. Brown acknowledges in passing that throughout history, *homo politicus* assumed "a masculinist comportment and sphere of activity." In other words, "*homo politicus* was almost always and expressly male." Brown, *Undoing the Demos*, 99. However, she holds that in "its popular-sovereignty variant today" it is less gendered than "*homo economicus* ever was." Brown, *Undoing the Demos*, 107.

49. Brown, *Edgework*, 106.

50. Ibid.

51. Ibid.

52. See, e.g., Lise Vogel, *Marxism and the Oppression of Women: Toward a Unitary Theory* (New Brunswick: Rutgers University Press, 1983).

53. Ibid., 151.

54. Sheila Rowbotham, *Woman's Consciousness, Man's World* (London: Verso, 2015), 104; Vogel, *Marxism and the Oppression*, 151.

55. Vogel refers to "child-bearing women," but it is important to recognize that this category, more specifically, refers here to those who are female-assigned-at-birth. While male pregnancy was deemed inconceivable until fairly recently, today there are men, trans/masculine individuals, and nonbinary individuals who get pregnant, give birth, chest feed, and parent children. In 2008, Thomas Beatie was the first legally defined male to give birth in North America.

56. By "statistical discrimination," economists refer to the idea that employers make employment decisions based on imperfect information concerning the applicants' productivity and therefore use statistical information on the group they belong to in order to infer productivity. In other words, if a group such as "women" is less productive statistically owing to the overall time they spend out of waged labor, each individual in this group will be assumed to be less productive.

57. This is not just a theoretical thought experiment but increasingly becomes a reality in many trans-affirming communities. As Loren Cannon writes (237), trans communities include pregnant dads and sperm-providing moms and "wombs, penises, sperm, and ovaries have been disconnected from the role and functions of motherhood and fatherhood." See Loren Cannon, "Firestonian Futures and Trans-Affirming Presents," *Hypatia: Journal of Feminist Philosophy* 31, no. 2 (2016): 229–44.

58. Brown, *Edgework*, 106.

59. Ibid.

60. See, e.g., Cinzia Arruza, "From Social Reproduction Feminism to the Women's Strike," in *Social Reproduction Theory: Remapping Class, Recentering Oppression*, ed. Tithi Bhattacharya (London: Pluto Press, 2017), 192–96.

61. Zhivka Valiavicharska, "Introduction" (presentation at *Dispatches from Resistant Mexico: Screening and Discussion with Director Caitlin Manning*, Pratt Institute, February 12, 2019).

62. Wanda Vrasti, "Self-Reproducing Movements and the Enduring Challenge of Materialist Feminism," in *Scandalous Economics: Gender and the Politics of Financial Crises*, ed. Aida A. Hozic and Jacqui True (Oxford: Oxford University Press, 2016), 248–65.

120   63. The pitfalls of identity politics have been forcefully demonstrated by Wendy Brown. See, e.g., Wendy Brown, *States of Injury*. Asad Haider builds on Brown's work in his recent book, *Mistaken Identity*, which argues persuasively that a common interest cannot be built on a given identity but can only be constituted in a political process. See Asad Haider, *Mistaken Identity: Race and Class in the Age of Trump* (London: Verso, 2018), 50.

CHAPTER 7

Four Concepts in Depoliticized Politics

Asad Haider

A dizzying shift from neoliberalism to a new authoritarian populism seems to frame the contemporary moment, from the Trump election in the United States to the rise of comparable right-wing movements across Europe and Latin America. Wendy Brown's analysis of neoliberalism in *Undoing the Demos*, followed by her recent work on this strange sequence, which culminates in *In the Ruins of Neoliberalism*, represents an invaluable point of reference for the political analysis of the present.

Looking out at the contemporary conjuncture, or the current "contingent genealogical formation," Brown asks, "What generates the anti-political yet libertarian *and* authoritarian dimensions of popular right-wing reaction today?"[1] So we are dealing with a seemingly political phenomenon that is fundamentally *antipolitical*—it is constituted by "the displacement of the social and attack on the political, along with the broad discrediting of democratic norms," which has "fueled and legitimated energies emanating from an entirely different set of concrete neoliberal effects." The "energies of aggrieved power" emanating from "men, whites, Christianity, and nation-states," targeting "politicians, liberal elites, immigrants, Muslims, Jews, queers, Blacks . . . would not have a legitimate political form in a liberal or social democratic order, which is why they remained on the political fringe until recent years." But these phenomena are not a reversal of the political coordinates of the preceding period—indeed, "neoliberal reason's assault on egalitarianism, social provision, social justice, politics, and democracy, along with its extension of the 'personal, protected sphere,' [the reference is to Hayek] has given them that legitimate form."[2] To try to understand these phenomena in the pre-neoliberal terms of "populism, authoritarianism, fascism" would not be adequate in capturing "the strange brew of bellicosity, disinhibition, and an anti-democratic blend of license and support for statism in current political and social formations." These terms, Brown argues, fail to "identify the specific elements of neoliberal reason—a radically extended reach of the private, mistrust of the political and disavowal of the social, which together normalize inequality and disembowel democracy—that shape and legitimize these angry white right political passions."[3]

Yet there is clearly something else, something more than neoliberalism, to understand. As Brown adds, "Neoliberal reason by itself, including its rollout in law and policy, and its interpellation of subjects, does not generate nationalist movements hell-bent on whitening nations, walling out immigrants and refugees, or vilifying feminists, queers, liberals, leftists, intellectuals, and even mainstream journalists." This, for Brown, requires understanding not only a "*logic* of governing reasons," but also "the affective energies giving shape and content to contemporary rightist political formations and expressions."[4]

In an effort to understand Brown's problematic, the structuring questions and terms that underlie her diagnosis, we will examine four concepts, which play varying roles in Brown's work and in the work that is in constellation around it.

1. DEPOLITICIZATION

To understand the antipolitical, we will begin with depoliticization. In her analysis of tolerance in *Regulating Aversion*, Brown outlines many features of the phenomenon of depoliticization, which "involves construing inequality, subordination, marginalization, and social conflict, which all require political analysis and political solutions, as personal and individual, on the one hand, or as natural, religious, or cultural on the other." Furthermore, depoliticization removes "a political phenomenon from comprehension of its historical emergence and from a recognition of the powers that produce and contour it." In all of its forms, depoliticization "eschews power and history in the representation of its subject. When these two constitutive sources of social relations and political conflict are elided, an ontological naturalness or essentialism almost inevitably takes up residence in our understandings and explanations."[5]

This does not mean, however, that depoliticization is the ruse of the powerful. If we put things this way, we will be left prey to the misunderstanding, which Foucault criticized in the first volume of *The History of Sexuality*, "that one is always 'inside' power, there is no 'escaping' it, there is no absolute outside where it is concerned, because one is subject to the law in any case." For this view, "history being the ruse of reason, power is the ruse of history, always emerging the winner." Foucault pointed out that "this would be to misunderstand the strictly relational character of power relationships."[6]

Consistent with Foucault's critique, Brown distances herself from the view of depoliticization as a "scheme" that would be "traceable to the interests of a dominant political group." Yet, nevertheless, depoliticization "does conserve the status quo and dissimulates the powers that organize it":

> The depoliticization entailed in liberalism, American political culture, and neoliberal rationality discussed in this study involves casting the existing order of things as inevitable, natural, or accidental rather than as the issue of orders or networks of power that privilege some at the expense of others. Thus depoliticization serves the powerful, but that service does not mean that the powerful intentionally and consciously develop and deploy this strategy to shore up their position. To the contrary, depoliticization may well issue from a certain blindness about power and dominance that is the privilege of the powerful. . . . This notion of a profound power effect absent a master choreographer but correspondent to the standpoint of the dominant is consonant not just with Marx's argument about the emergence of political ideology in the *German Ideology* but also

with Foucault's account of the emergence of certain discourses of power in *The Order of Things, Discipline and Punish*, and *The History of Sexuality*, vol. 1.[7]

We will return to this problem of power and this range of theoretical references, but first we should return to the present. Brown's work shows how the enabling condition for right-wing anti-politics has been depoliticization. We can understand depoliticization in the historically specific terms of the neoliberal category of governance, which "reconceives the political as a field of management or administration."[8] "The discourse and practice of governance," Brown writes, "depoliticizes its own deployment and field of application."[9] In its actual practice, "governance disseminates a depoliticizing epistemology, ontology, and set of practices. Soft, inclusive, and technical in orientation, governance buries contestable norms and structural striations (such as class), as well as the norms and exclusions circulated by its procedures and decisions. It integrates subjects into the purposes and trajectories of the nations, firms, universities, or other entities employing it. In public life, governance displaces liberal democratic-justice concerns with technical formulations of problems, questions of right with questions of efficiency, even questions of legality with those of efficacy."[10] If we were to join Brown's contemporary critique with the critical theory of late capitalism, we might say that neoliberal depoliticization continues the trend of the foreclosure of politics by technocratic and bureaucratic exclusion of the public from the various forms and practices characteristic of representative democracy. But this problem of depoliticization appears in a new light with the emergence of the extreme Right "in the ruins of neoliberalism." Here right-wing populism appears to be a kind of repoliticization, or even hyperpoliticization.[11] But the antipolitical, or perhaps pseudopolitical reaction of the Right, despite appearing to be a repoliticization, is in fact complicit with neoliberal depoliticization. It would be mistaken to see right-wing authoritarianism, as liberals frequently do, as a hyperpoliticization. This fails to perceive the complicity between neoliberalism and right-wing authoritarianism, and thus urges further depoliticization.

From this vantage point, there is little more in the political land-scape than depoliticization in various forms, often appearing to be pseudopoliticization; all of these forms of depoliticization seem to generate each other and falsely claim to respond to each other. Contemporary critical theory, in line with Brown, might set out to offer a diagnosis of pseudopoliticization but within a theoretical framework that refers to the possibility of radical democracy, understood in terms of plurality and contingency rather than a unitary and essentialist foundation, with a range of subject positions entering into political contestation and participation.[12] The plurality of subject positions is a conception of the political that by definition opposes the anti-politics that appears as hyperpoliticization, in the sense that the latter is in fact the erasure of politics through its grounding of the community in a largely ethno-national bond, named by populism as the people. Against such anti-politics, the plurality of subject positions requires institutionalization as radical democracy.

Now, we can conceive of the problem of depoliticization in historical terms—the rise of the rationality of neoliberalism—but also in conceptual terms that are at stake in this historical change. In other words, Brown's work also invites us to understand depoliticization not as a historical shift but as a constitutive concept. What is at stake is not only an analysis of the present but also the very definition of politics and the political.

What does it mean to think the political through depoliticization? Brown's commentary on depoliticization is woven in with her long-standing engagement with Marx, who in *Undoing the Demos* is frequently contrasted to Foucault, yet nevertheless remains a decisive reference for understanding depoliticization as a foundational process in the modern formation of the political. In her analysis of Marx's "On the Jewish Question" in *States of Injury*, Brown writes:

Marx is again underscoring how certain modalities of social and economic domination are less eliminated than *depoliticized* by the political revolutions heralding formal equality, although these modalities are transformed in the process, losing their formal representation in the state as estates. At the same time, Marx is seeking to articulate the extent to which the modern *individual* is produced by and through, indeed *as*, this depoliticization and in the image of it. He is proffering a political genealogy of the sovereign individual, whose crucial site of production is the depoliticization of social relations. Put the other way around, Marx exposes the modern formulation of sovereignty as itself a modality of discursive depoliticization.[13]

That is, the separation of the economic and the political that is constitutive of capitalism enacts a broad depoliticization and produces individuals as subjects who are subjected to depoliticized powers.

Parallel to this analysis is another framework for understanding the constitution of the political as depoliticization. It is the feminist critique of liberalism, also advanced in *States of Injury*:

Women doing primary labor and achieving primary identity inside the family are thus inherently constrained in their prospects for recognition as persons insofar as they lack the stuff of liberal personhood—legal, economic, or civil personality. They are derivative of their households and husbands, subsumed in identity to their maternal activity, and sequestered from the place where rights are exercised, wages are earned, and political power is wielded. Moreover, because the liberal state does not recognize the family as a political entity or reproduction as a social relation, women's situation as unpaid workers within the family is depoliticized.[14]

Note that a fundamental feature of depoliticization is the exclusion of women from the political, tied up with the unremunerated character of the reproductive activities of women in the household and the failure of the state to recognize these activities. We will return to this problem of reproduction, but for now we will focus on the problem of the political.

We can understand depoliticization as a mutually constitutive process with the formation of the political. From this Foucauldian and feminist vantage point, depoliticization is fundamentally gendered: it represents the constitutive outside of the political sphere, especially those gendered activities that are not counted as political and thus produce the space of the political.[15] More specifically, this is the outside of the self-interested and self-oriented male subject of liberalism, with women confined to the set of activities marked as "feminine" within the gendered division of labor that facilitates the autonomy of the male subject. The possibility of power struggles in the space excluded from the political is foreclosed. As Brown writes in *Edgework*, "for many feminists, the legal and political concept of privacy is a highly ambivalent one insofar as, historically, 'the private' has functioned to depoliticize many of the constituent activities and injuries of women—reproduction and caring for children, domestic violence, incest, unremunerated household labor, emotional and sexual service to men."[16]

We are faced then with two different, perhaps opposing, understandings not only of depoliticization but consequently of the political. First, it is the space that has an affinity for democracy, which must be institutionalized and whose institutions must be defended against antipolitical tendencies. Second, it is the space that is constituted by the exclusion of the values and practices that may be the site of social struggles.

2. SUBJECT

As Brown shows in *Politics Out of History*, depoliticization is also fundamentally tied up with the closure of political horizons, a reality that is difficult to confront, owing perhaps to certain psychic habits of melancholia:

> In the left tradition from Marx to Marcuse, the presumption of a subject born with a passion for freedom—self-realizing in work and self-legislating in society—is also unquestioned, no matter how fraught the path to gaining that freedom. A counterpoint to this modernist confidence in the desire for freedom is offered by the line of thought that runs from Nietzsche to Weber, cresting

in Foucault's theory of subjectivization. But have we faced the extent to which this counterpoint depletes a crucial source of the progressivist vision, rooted not in the rationality of the liberal state or in the reasoning capacities of the modernist subject, but in the nature of the liberal subject's desire itself?[17]

This important reference to Marcuse will recur in our reading, and in *Edgework* Brown lays out the consequences of this depletion: "Without another conscious vantage point from which to perceive, criticize, and counter present arrangements, a vantage point Herbert Marcuse argued largely vanished in postwar capitalism, it is almost impossible to sustain a radical vision as realistic or as livable."[18] More specifically, as Brown argues throughout *Undoing the Demos*, there is a fundamental vision that the young Marx shares with a long tradition revolving around *homo politicus*. Revisiting her study of "On the Jewish Question," Brown writes that "the importance of homo *politicus* in modern political thought explains . . . Marx's obsession in his early writings with the unrealized figure of sovereign political man and with his critique of the compromised status of political man in constitutional democracy."[19] This leads us to the problem of the political subject: "If Marx's analysis remains unequaled in its account of capitalism's power, imperatives, brutality and world-making capacities, this analysis also presumed subjects who yearned for emancipation and had at hand a political idiom of justice—unrealized principles of democracy—through which to demand it. These subjects and principles can be presumed no longer."[20] In *Undoing the Demos*, the problem of the subject revolves around the division between *homo oeconomicus* and *homo politicus*. Neoliberalism, depoliticization, and governance are all caught up with the displacement of *homo politicus*, the fundamentally democratic subject, by *homo oeconomicus*. Now the political subject appears to be absent. And indeed, the power of the preceding conceptions of the political can be considered by raising the problem of the subject.

What is the subject that can become political? On the basis of the foregoing critique of the political, we could first advance a normative democratic conception that opposes to the "people" of populism a plurality of heterogeneous subject positions that cannot be confined within national borders. This subject must be institutionalized, in the sense that there are formalized political procedures to protect this plurality and secure participation, thus responding not only to the horizontalism of social movements but also to their elaboration of new institutions. 129 Second, we could point to a proliferation of social struggles that challenge the line drawn between the political and the depoliticized space of the margins. These struggles demonstrate, for example, the gendered exploitation of the household and show that the power relations in this space are political. Third, we could point to *homo politicus* as the foundation of politics: "the creature who rules itself and rules as part of the demos."[21] It is "a subject of politics, a demotic subject, which cannot be reduced to right, interest, individual security, or individual advantage, although of course these features everywhere dapple its landscape and language in modernity. This subject, *homo politicus*, forms the substance and legitimacy of whatever democracy might mean beyond securing the individual provisioning of individual ends; this 'beyond' includes political equality and freedom, representation, popular sovereignty, and deliberation and judgment about the public good and the common."[22] Each of these positions is a real effect of the foregoing analysis. Yet viewed as a foundation for the political, *homo politicus* sits uneasily alongside the plurality of subject positions or the power struggles of those who are excluded from it in the moment of its constitution.

We are forced to ask, recalling Brown, whether our definitions of the political can avoid the fate of repeating what is contained in depoliticization: "an ontological naturalness or essentialism." At this stage, we cannot avoid returning to the mutually constitutive character of the formation of the political and depoliticization: insofar as there is an inside/outside relation of *homo politicus* and the excluded feminine, familial subjects, can these "outside" subjects in fact serve as the basis for an emancipatory political subjectivity? In other words, can an emancipatory political subject actually rest on the foundation of a subject that is itself defined as the outside of *homo politicus* and thus also constituted by *homo politicus*? Is this an invention of new subjectivities or a repetition of subjectivities subjected to *homo politicus*?

Brown shows that for Foucault, the notion of "political rationality," which is at play in the analysis of neoliberalism, develops the relational theory of power and thus "always comes in a particular form, secures and circulates specific norms, and posits particular subjects and relations."[23] In other words, power relations are constitutive of political subjects, and to think of a subjectivity that is not subjected to existing powers means either identifying a prior foundation or finding a way to conceive of new subjects emerging and breaking from what exists.

Generally restated, our question is whether subjects defined by their plurality and heterogeneity, or their disavowal and exclusion, constitute an emancipatory politics. If indeed depoliticization and exclusion both operate according to a kind of feedback loop, is it not necessary to conceive of emancipatory subjects that are in excess of the existing situation—that is, that posit different ways of thinking what is possible? These different "possibles" would constitute politics in the multiple rather than a domain of the political, and these multiple politics would take on different modes in different specific, historical situations.[24]

Here we encounter a limit to existing social movements, together with neoliberalism or the rise of the Right. Whether social movements have been horizontalist and pluralist or based on a coalition of marginal subjectivities, they have not managed to advance modes of acting politically that respond to the specificity of our current situation. If we understand political subjectivity as what allows us to go beyond that which exists, this presents us with a different way to understand depoliticization: not as incursions into democratic institutions or the exclusion of other practices of social life, but rather as the obsolescence of existing political processes. That is, to conceive of different modes of politics implies identifying political forms and practices that are not measured according to democratic norms, however conceived, but according to their potential for the constitution of new subjectivities.

3. REPRODUCTION

An alternative to the political subjectivity of *homo politicus* can be found in the theories of social reproduction and the feminist struggles related to it. As Cinzia Arruzza writes in a lucid analysis of the concept, which both acknowledges its fundamental complexity and defends it from extrinsic criticisms: "The notion of social reproduction within the framework of a unitary theory enables us to understand the current crisis not simply in economistic terms, but rather as a general crisis of the reproduction of capitalist society considered in all of its dimensions. Moreover, it enables us to understand why neoliberal globalization and the current crisis are leading to an increasing privatization and commodification of social reproduction, with capital penetrating into spheres that in the past were not directly subsumed by the market."[25]

In this historical situation, the concept of reproduction is indispensable. However, its polysemy poses the risk that the explanatory power of the term may exceed the delimited space within which it can operate in its specificity (we shall encounter a similar dilemma in the word "repression"). Indeed, the broader range of possible meanings, which are frequently irreconcilable, is not dissipated by more precise formulations; these other meanings have discursive and practical effects. With no claim to comprehensiveness, I will describe four possible definitions, which seem to coexist implicitly in the term, frequently blurring into each other and modifying each other in important ways.

1. The reproduction of biological life through activities that exist across every form of society (meaning that there is an "intuitive" distinction between activities such as building machine tools and cooking meals, and thus the "intuitive" gendering of this distinction).

2. The reproduction of the conditions of existence for any mode of production (meaning that there is a transhistorical imperative to meet subsistence needs through activities corresponding to the transhistorical categories of labor and production or even capital).

3. The reproduction of capitalist societies (meaning that subsistence needs are met through the allocation of the total social capital rather than production at the household level, and therefore that building machine tools is part of social reproduction, since it is required for the production of consumer goods).

4. The reproduction of labor power through nonwaged activity (meaning that the supposedly natural, feminized work situated in the

household is actually generated by capitalist relations of production, which separate activities that were historically not necessarily distinguished sexually or even spatially).

132

In this partial list of definitions, which are by no means adopted in any unitary manner in any discourse on social reproduction, the first two meanings are transhistorical and the second two historically specific, but not in the same ways.

The last, most specific definition powerfully points to the gendered conditions for capitalist accumulation. It is thus perhaps not surprising that it has so frequently led to debates over whether reproductive work is productive of value, debates that are in some sense scholastic but also force us to think through the basic categories of the economic. We can illustrate the problem in less technical terms. If a can is filled with food in a factory and the food is emptied into a pot at home, where is the line between production and reproduction? If a male worker is paid a wage and his wife goes shopping with a portion of that wage, where is the line between waged and unwaged work?

Such problems can quite easily be waved away if we simply resort to the ideological intuitions of the transhistorical definitions. With the intuition about the gendered character of the reproduction of biological life, lines can be drawn between different forms of activity that determine some as production and others as reproduction. With the transhistorical conception of the reproduction of the conditions of existence of any society, a broad spectrum of human activity, including what is not usually counted as labor, can be granted the status of anthropological necessity. The ambiguity of the categories used to understand the historically specific conditions for the reproduction of capitalist society is thus resolved with a biological and anthropological foundation. As Arruzza points out, this ideological guarantee is secured by "turning sexual biological difference into an explanatory *deus ex machina*," while "it is exactly the social meaning attributed to that difference that needs to be explained."[26] What this would mean is a return to that other foundationalist figuration of the human, to *homo economicus* and its obverse, as Brown has it in *Undoing the Demos*, of *femina domestica*.[27]

There is a sense in which such a resort to ideological intuitions can provide a quasi-physiological guarantee for the anti-capitalist character of feminism—just as the metaphysics of labor and of class have provided such guarantees within Marxism. But we must now ask whether feminist struggles, and indeed any other anti-capitalist struggles, require such a guarantee. Does a coalitional struggle require this physiological substratum? To what extent do questions of feminist struggle have to be related to the capitalist mode of production in order for socialist-feminist struggle to be possible? Is it indeed necessary to provide a proof of the value-productivity of housework, as the Wages for Housework movement constantly debated?

The specificity of reproduction returns us to the problem of the political subject: Can we conceive of an emancipatory politics against the totality of the social structure without deriving the emancipatory subject from the analysis of the social structure itself? Now, the search for foundations is by no means specific to arguments around social reproduction, and as we have pointed out, the theory itself requires no such foundationalism. But the metaphysics of labor and class have yielded in themselves ideological foundationalisms, which can be dramatically illustrated by the example of a chapter of Marcuse's *Essay on Liberation*, "A Biological Foundation for Socialism." We now turn to Brown's use of Marcuse and the status of this foundation.

4. REPRESSION

"Certainly *ressentiment* is a vital energy of right-wing populism," Brown writes. "Rancor, grudges, barely concealed victimization, and other affects of *reaction* are the affective heartbeat of internet trolling, tweets, and speeches at right-wing rallies, and a striking feature of Trump's own demeanor."[28] Building on Nietzsche's canonical analysis of ressentiment, Brown presents an analysis of right-wing populism as nihilism. Crucial as a historicizing gesture is the way Brown relates the Nietzschean terminology to Marcuse's Marxist and Freudian account of repressive desublimation. In Brown's interpretation: "What Marcuse famously termed 'repressive desublimation' occurs within an order of capitalist domination, exploitation and 'false needs' as technology reduces the demands of necessity and desire is everywhere incorporated into a commodity culture enjoyed by a growing middle class. This order features plenty of pleasure, including that obtained by radically reduced strictures on sexuality (less grueling work requires less sublimation), but not emancipation. Instinctual energies, rather than being directly opposed by the mandates of society and economy, and thus requiring heavy repression and sublimation, are now coopted by and for capitalist production and marketing."[29] This argument, as Brown points out, is quite familiar. But to develop an analysis of right-wing nihilism, Brown traces Marcuse's analysis of repressive desublimation to his notion of a "happy consciousness," which resolves "the conflict between desire and social requirements by aligning one's consciousness with the regime."[30] The result, according to Brown: "As late capitalist desublimation relaxes demands against the instincts but does not free the subject for self-direction, demands for intellection are substantially relaxed. Free, stupid, manipulable, absorbed by if not addicted to trivial stimuli and gratifications, the subject of repressive desublimation in advanced capitalist society is not just libidinally unbound, released to enjoy more pleasure, but released from more general expectations of social conscience and social comprehension. This release is amplified by the neoliberal assault on the social and the depression of conscience fostered by nihilism."[31] While nihilism and happy consciousness are the original and salient features of Brown's analysis of the contemporary right, the initial two terms, which form the scaffolding of the elaborated argument, are worth revisiting. Here we focus on repressive desublimation. The relation of Marcuse's psychoanalytic and Marxist theory invites comparison to the Foucauldian framework of *Undoing the Demos*. An amusing remark by Marcuse in a 1977 interview serves as a useful entry point into the problem:

> According to Marx, "alienation" was a socio-economic concept, and it meant, basically (this is a very brutal abbreviation), that under Capitalism men and women could not, in their work, fulfil their own individual human faculties and needs; that this was

due to the capitalist mode of production itself; and that it could be remedied only by radically changing this mode of production. Now today, the concept of alienation has been expanded to such an extent that this original content is almost entirely lost; it has been applied to all sorts of psychological troubles. But not every kind of trouble or problem someone has, for example with his or her girlfriend or boyfriend, is necessarily due to the capitalist mode of production.[32]

Marcuse's interesting point is that the concept of alienation has been overextended. But here the word "alienation" remains an epistemological obstacle, symptomatic of Marcuse's mode of reading Marx. We might reframe his compelling criticism by proposing that in fact *the explanatory power of alienation is too great*, because of an ambiguity intrinsic to the concept. This ambiguity may be understood as a lack, a lack which requires a Freudian supplement. The problem, then, with "repressive desublimation" as a concept is that it is founded on the overextension of the concept of alienation, which relies on the humanist subject as foundation and therefore must understand different sexual moralities not in terms of the productive and relational character of power but rather as byproducts of different modes of labor under the rubric of the repressive hypothesis.

I count two direct references to Marcuse in the first volume of the *History of Sexuality*, which appeared precisely the year before this interview with Marcuse. While Marcuse is not named, the allusions are unmistakable. Foucault refers first to a theory that attempts to periodize sexual repression and identify its mode of operating in a period of late capitalism. According to the narrative Foucault is criticizing, late capitalism is a period "in which the exploitation of wage labor does not demand the same violent and physical constraints as in the nineteenth century, and where the politics of the body does not require the elision of sex or its restriction solely to the reproductive function; it relies instead on a multiple channeling into the controlled circuits of the economy—on what has been called a hyperrepressive desublimation."[33] But this attempt at periodization is precisely what demonstrates the internal limit of the concept of repression. Foucault concludes: "If the politics of sex makes little use of the law of the taboo but brings into play an entire technical machinery, if what is involved is the production of sexuality rather than the repression of sex, then our emphasis has to be placed elsewhere; we must shift our analysis away from the problem of 'labor capacity' and doubtless abandon the diffuse energetics that underlies the theme of a sexuality repressed for economic reasons."[34] So I believe our first question is whether we can understand the affective basis of right-wing populism and authoritarianism in the language of repressive desublimation without reproducing various contentious terms: an ontology of labor, the humanist subject, historicism / expressive causality, and the repressive hypothesis.

Second, I will point to the very famous lines of Foucault on "the strictly relational character of power relationships," immediately following the lines quoted earlier. He writes:

> Their existence depends on a multiplicity of points of resistance: these play the role of adversary, target, support, or handle in power relations. These points of resistance are present everywhere in the power network. Hence there is no single locus of great Refusal, no soul of revolt, source of all rebellions, or pure law of the revolutionary. Instead there is a plurality of resistances, each of them a special case: resistances that are possible, necessary, improbable; others that are spontaneous, savage, solitary, concerted, rampant, or violent; still others that are quick to compromise, interested, or sacrificial; by definition, they can only exist in the strategic field of power relations.[35]

The Great Refusal, however, is polysemic in Marcuse's own reference. In *One-Dimensional Man*, the Great Refusal is identified at the level of the aesthetic, with a tragic conclusion regarding the character of the text itself: "The critical theory of society possesses no concepts which could bridge the gap between the present and its future; holding no promise and showing no success, it remains negative. Thus it wants to remain loyal to those who, without hope, have given and give their life to the Great Refusal."[36] But in the 1969 preface to *An Essay on Liberation*, Mar-

136

cuse includes in the Great Refusal not only the student movements of 1968 but also the revolutions of Vietnam, Cuba, and China. Of the student radicals he writes that "in proclaiming . . . the Great Refusal, they recognize the mark of social repression."[37] In this context the Great Refusal is explained according to its biological and moral dimensions:

> Political radicalism thus implies moral radicalism: the emergence of a morality which might precondition man for freedom. This radicalism activates the elementary, organic foundation of morality in the human being. Prior to all ethical behavior in accordance with specific social standards, prior to all ideological expression, morality is a "disposition" of the organism, perhaps rooted in the erotic drive to counter aggressiveness, to create and preserve "ever greater unities" of life. We would then have, this side of all "values," an instinctual foundation for solidarity among human beings—a solidarity which has been effectively repressed in line with the requirements of class society but which now appears as a precondition for liberation.[38]

The Freudian references to instincts, drives, and "ever greater unities" run parallel to the solidarity and overcoming of class society, together constituting a foundation for liberation. Marcuse goes on:

> To the degree to which this foundation is itself historical and the malleability of "human nature" reaches into the depth of man's instinctual structure, changes in morality may "sink down" into the "biological" dimension and modify organic behavior. Once a specific morality is firmly established as a norm of social behavior, it is not only introjected—it also operates as a norm of "organic" behavior: the organism receives and reacts to certain stimuli and "ignores" and repels others in accord with the introjected morality, which is thus promoting or impeding the function of the organism as a living cell in the respective society. In this way, a society constantly re-creates, this side of consciousness and ideology, patterns of behavior and aspiration as part of

the "nature" of its people, and unless the revolt reaches into this "second" nature, into these ingrown patterns, social change will remain "incomplete," even self-defeating.[39]

Now, with Foucault we are very distant from the libidinal foundation of revolt. From the critique of a periodization of repression—whether it rests on a "material" basis of the economy or not—we have the argument for the productive and relational character of power. Within this theory of power we have the argument for strategic resistances rather than revolt resting on a unitary foundation. But what then is the basis for a political subject that can change what exists? With Marcuse, we have a foundationalist theory of the subject, whether the languages of morality, nature, and biology are to be taken literally or not. With Foucault, on the other hand, we have the proliferation of resistances, modified by a range of adjectives (spontaneous, savage, solitary . . .). It is not clear, however, that these resistances are capable of, or even aspire to, changing the structured and stubborn status quo.

It would not be difficult to make an argument against a biological foundation for socialism; more essential is to make the argument against any foundation whatsoever, since the foundations available to us are embedded in what already exists. How then do we speak of a political subject that is anti-capitalist and subsequently anti-neoliberal and anti-authoritarian? This question remains open.

From the vantage point of the possible, subjects do not rest on foundations, but they are real and can be observed in those infrequent moments when a challenge to the existing order appears. Outside of these moments, political behaviors and consciousnesses, if studied with reference to a foundation, will generally be found wanting. And it is beyond doubt that some will not only be undesirable but also repellent, harmful, and dangerous. It would be interesting here to move back from the reference to Nietzsche to Spinoza, for whom "sad passions," such as anger, hatred, and envy, are caused by the inability to act. There is nothing of an "excuse" for right-wing affects in this but rather a recognition of the bleak reality that there are few ways for people to act politically. Such sad passions are not the monopoly of the Right but are also to be found on the Left. To study them may require a new theory of the subject. One of the most valuable contributions of Brown's work is to show how the various regimes of neoliberal and authoritarian subjectivity have both enabled and constrained theories of the subject.

NOTES

1. Wendy Brown, "Neoliberalism's Frankenstein: Authoritarian Freedom in Twenty-First Century 'Democracies,'" *Critical Times: Interventions in Global Critical Theory* 1, no. 1 (2018): 61, 67.
2. Ibid., 67.
3. Ibid.
4. Ibid., 68; emphasis in original.
5. Wendy Brown, *Regulating Aversion: Tolerance in the Age of Identity and Empire* (Princeton: Princeton University Press, 2006), 15.
6. Michel Foucault, *The History of Sexuality*, trans. Robert Hurley, vol. 1 (New York: Pantheon, 1978), 95.
7. Brown, *Regulating Aversion*, 211–12.
8. Wendy Brown, *Undoing the Demos: Neoliberalism's Stealth Revolution* (New York: Zone Books, 2017), 127.
9. Ibid., 130.
10. Ibid., 131.
11. On the questions of depoliticization and repoliticization, I am indebted to the argument of Robin Celikates, which is outlined in his contribution to this volume.
12. See again Celikates.
13. Wendy Brown, *States of Injury: Power and Freedom in Late Modernity* (Princeton: Princeton University Press, 1995), 112.
14. Ibid., 182.
15. Here I am indebted to the argument of Johanna Oksala, outlined in her contribution to this volume.
16. Wendy Brown, *Edgework: Critical Essays on Knowledge and Politics* (Princeton: Princeton University Press, 2009), 128.
17. Wendy Brown, *Politics Out of History* (Princeton: Princeton University Press, 2001), 47.
18. Brown, *Edgework*, 107.
19. Brown, *Undoing the Demos*, 206.
20. Ibid., 111.
21. Ibid., 41.
22. Ibid., 87.
23. Ibid., 115.
24. Sylvain Lazarus, *Anthropology of the Name*, trans. Gila Walker (New York: Seagull Books, 2015).
25. Cinzia Arruzza, "Functionalist, Determinist, Reductionist: Social Reproduction Feminism and Its Critics," *Science & Society* 80, no. 1 (December 16, 2015): 9–30, 11.

26. Ibid., 20.
27. Brown, *Undoing the Demos*, 99, 104.
28. Brown, "Neoliberalism's Frankenstein," 70.
29. Ibid., 72.
30. Ibid.
31. Ibid., 72–73.
32. Bryan Magee, *Talking Philosophy: Dialogues with Fifteen Leading Philosophers* (Oxford: Oxford University Press, 1978), 50–51.
33. Foucault, *The History of Sexuality*, vol. 1: *An Introduction*, trans. Robert Hurley (New York: Vintage, 1978), 114.
34. Ibid.
35. Ibid., 95–96.
36. Herbert Marcuse, *One-Dimensional Man: Studies in the Ideology of Advanced Industrial Society*, 2nd ed. (New York: Routledge, 1991), 261.
37. Herbert Marcuse, *An Essay on Liberation* (Boston: Beacon Press, 2000), ix.
38. Ibid., 10.
39. Ibid., 10–11.

CHAPTER 8

De-, Hyper-, or Pseudopoliticization?

Undoing and Remaking the Demos
in the Age of Right-Wing Authoritarianism

Robin Celikates

1. POLITICIZATION: BE CAREFUL WHAT YOU WISH FOR?

Until recently, leftist political commentators and theorists seemed primarily worried about depoliticization—the tendency that more and more important decisions were being taken by experts and bureaucrats behind closed doors, framed in terms of the TINA ("there is no alternative") principle and shielded from political participation and political contestation.[1] Picking up political tropes going back at least to the 1960s—and made prominent in, for example, the early work of Jürgen Habermas and his critique of the technocratic reframing of essentially practical questions as technical ones for which there is an expertise-based way to determine the right answer[2]—they would lament the rise or return of technocratic government and governance and the democracy-undermining effects this depoliticization "from above" would trigger. In this constellation, (re)politicization was the name of the game emancipatory countermovements were expected to play.

Today, in what seems a radically different political constellation, the worry has shifted. In recent years we all have heard former proponents of radical democracy resort to the quintessentially liberal warning concerning politicization: "Be careful what you wish for!" Now, instead of depoliticization, politicization or even hyperpoliticization has come to be seen as the signature of our age—variously designated as "the age of anger," "the populist moment," or the "new authoritarianism." Reacting against the socially engineered depoliticization associated with neoliberalism and the technocratic (and presumably cosmopolitan or multicultural) elites behind it, we seem to be witnessing a backlash that has taken the form of a massive repoliticization—not the one we may have been hoping for but one that fuses the mobilization of legitimating reactionary affects "from below" with hierarchically organized movements and parties and, in some cases, when they manage to win elections, government repression "from above."[3] Symbolically, this hazardous mélange culminated, most recently, in the storming of the US Capitol on January 6, 2021, by a mob wearing "MAGA Civil War" shirts, carrying nooses and gallows, and shouting treason. Apocalyptic and hysterical hyperpoliticization seemed to have turned ordinary citizens first into self-proclaimed revolutionaries and then into domestic terrorists on the run from the FBI. The insurrectionists could even appear as an—admittedly quixotic and unhinged—section of a countermovement reacting against the socially engineered depoliticization associated with neoliberalism and the technocratic elites behind it. In this context, the mantra of "taking back control" is just another, more anodyne name for what is often interpreted as a politicization of issues such as migration that have presumably been shielded from excessive popular "input" by liberal policy elites and those who helped them establish cultural hegemony.[4]

If this is a familiar narrative about the rise of right-wing parties and movements of a new type all over the Western world—if we indeed have entered a "new era of antidemocratic politics" propelled forward by and in turn weaponizing "reactionary populism, nativism, racism, and xenophobia"[5]—the equally familiar liberal reaction that recoils in horror at how hyperpoliticization strikes back and that frantically tries to reassemble the tools of depoliticization clearly falls short. As Wendy Brown's masterful analysis of "Neoliberalism's Stealth Revolution" in *Undoing the Demos* and the expansion of this analysis in her most recent writings—especially in *In the Ruins of Neoliberalism*—show, the liberal reaction falls short in at least two ways: It fails to understand both *that* it was precisely the neoliberal "mistrust of the political and disavowal of the social"[6] that fed into the rising right-wing authoritarianism and *how* the latter inherits this mistrust and disavowal in ways that combine superficial opposition to it with reproducing its deep logic of economization-cum-familialization in mutating combinations of neoliberal, traditionalist, nationalist, racist, and protectionist imaginaries and policies.[7] As a result, liberalism not only fails to recognize the intimate connection between neoliberalism and the right-wing backlash, it also mischaracterizes the latter by misreading it as a form of (hyper) politicization and then turns to the pseudosolution of further depoliticization, feeding back into the vicious circle it failed to see in the first place.

143

In what follows, I will build on Brown's diagnosis of the neoliberal program of "undoing the demos" and the right-wing reaction to it, and propose to distinguish between different forms of depoliticization and repoliticization that complicate contemporary discourses of populism. On the surface, both left-wing movements such as Occupy and more recent right-wing movements in Europe and the United States seem to respond to the neoliberal evacuation of the political by employing strategies of hyperpoliticization. As a result, commentators such as Colin Crouch equated populist movements—both left and right—in terms of their politicizing effect, presenting them as potential "refreshments for democracy" that would pose symmetrical threats to democracy if not suitably mediated.[8] Against such symmetrical interpretations, which find their troubling political counterpart in mainstream strategies that have significantly shifted the boundaries of acceptable political discourse and practice toward the extreme Right, while at the same time dismissing the radical claims of emancipatory and progressive political struggles and movements, I will argue that right-wing populism is better understood as mobilizing a dynamic of pseudopoliticization. Bringing Brown's work into conversation with recent analyses by Éric Fassin and others, I will show how this pseudopoliticization is ultimately antipolitical not just in virtue of its "content" but also of its "form." It therefore ends up contributing to the further "undoing of the demos" rather than to its "remaking." After saying a bit more about the dialectic of de- and repoliticization and how one might diagnose the traps of pseudopoliticization without relying on a perfectionist or essentialist notion of politics no longer tenable today, I will return to the scene of politicization "from the left" and sketch some implications for the debate about "left populism" and the problem of political form, before ending with even more rudimentary remarks on what a radical-democratic remaking of the demos—a remaking that also presupposes an undoing, albeit a different one—might look like.

First, then, let me return to the diagnosis—the *Zeitdiagnose*—of our age as one of hyperpoliticization. By calling our attention to the simultaneity (or only slightly deferred sequence) of the neoliberal "dethroning of the political" in neoliberalism and the "open politicization of the state"[9] as well as of religions values, traditions, morality, and mass affect[10] at the heart of the right-wing mobilizations of an angry people, Brown confronts us with the questions of whether and how different logics of depoliticization, politicization, and repoliticization can be accounted for theoretically without falling back into problematic essentialist or even ontological assumptions about the political.

While the depoliticizing logic of neoliberalism is straightforward enough and clearly analyzed in *Undoing the Demos*, "Neoliberalism's Frankenstein," and *In the Ruins of Neoliberalism*, the exact way in which "the open politicization" advocated by right-wing movements and parties is at the same time depoliticizing and indeed antipolitical calls for further elucidation. One element of a response is provided in the claim that these movements are "antipolitical" insofar as "they tend to denounce whatever goes by the name of conventional politics—its processes, compromises, institutions, and deliberative spaces,"[11] but this can be no more than a starting point if the radical-democratic claim still holds that politics necessarily exceeds what is conventionally understood as politics (its institutionally and formally determined and constrained constituted forms). It does, however, already point to an important feature of pseudopoliticization—namely, the desire to abandon and overcome all forms of mediation, self-restraint, and self-reflexivity, and just to "rule" (the German verb *durchregieren* more forcefully captures this dimension of the desire to rule without being hampered by tedious hindrances). This desire is itself depoliticizing, and ultimately antipolitical, as it curtails, undermines, and ultimately destroys the basis of politics—the possibility and legitimacy of political conflict and contestation. It is an "anti-politics" precisely because it releases and expresses "a ferocious will to power in politics"[12] that is unable and unwilling to constrain itself in the face of a plurality of political subject positions and lines of conflict that it sees as either an external threat or an internal weakness that needs to be eliminated. And it can only do so in a way that seems legitimate and necessary to many because it flows from the claim to speak and act in the name of the "true people," its moral identity and traditional values, or just to follow the logic of the game of hegemonic claim-making.

145

Analyzing apparent hyperpoliticization as ultimately antipolitical pseudopoliticization need not resort to a full-blown perfectionist or essentialist notion of politics as might be attributed to Arendt (who valorizes a certain collective enactment of freedom in public—although there are more and less essentializing readings of her account of the logic of political action). Rather, such an analysis only presupposes the "thin" assumption that the political dimension of life is tied to the possibility of political conflict and contestation (also and especially about the boundaries of the demos), and that these are in turn tied to the persistence of political power relations in historically variable forms. Politics presupposes a space of (genuine) political alternatives, and as a result political decisions can never be simply deduced from facts or expert opinions. Presumably pre- or extrapolitical cultural, historical, ethnic, and so on determinations of the political community therefore stand in contradiction to this fundamental logic of politics that necessarily opens up an underdetermined space for political conflict and contestation.

This understanding thus tries to occupy a conceptual ground beyond the unsatisfying dichotomy of an ahistorical and essentialist notion of the political, on the one hand, and a position that regards the political as nothing more than the contingent and historically variable outcome of struggles of politicization, on the other. On this view, it is precisely the open-endedness and indeterminacy of the political, the inability to draw its boundaries in any clear and lasting sense, that is the characteristic of the political.

Against this foil, the idea that these power relations and thus the reality of and need for political conflict can ultimately be overcome by grounding the political community in a pre- and extrapolitical bond that is culturally, historically, or ethnically specified—a bond that is seen as clearly demarcating the community and establishing its boundaries beyond any doubt—appears as the linchpin of the anti-politics of the contemporary moment, directed against democracy as the political order whose "legitimacy is drawn from exclusively political vocabularies and ordinances."[13]

I read Brown's insistence on learning from "Marx's fatal flaw"— namely, his "neglect of the enduring complexities of political power" and the way it mirrors neoliberalism's "inadequate appreciation of the political, and especially state, powers that would take shape in the wake of dismantled democratic restraints"[14]—as well as her reference to how this dimension was recognized as inextinguishable in the work of theorists of the political from Machiavelli via Schmitt (with qualifications) to Sheldon Wolin, as a basis for analyzing how what looks like hyperpoliticization is in fact not only illiberal and antidemocratic but also antipolitical.[15] In the end, it has little to offer in terms of countering the dual neoliberal displacement of the social and the political by a combination of markets and traditionalist morals. Instead of genuinely political actors, forms of agency, and practices, it only manages to conjure phantasmatic collectives (the true Americans or Germans) and various forms of *Ersatzhandeln*: the pseudo-action and acting out exemplified in the storming of the US Capitol. It literally "has nothing else,"[16] at least nothing else that could count as political or would establish a political alternative to the depoliticizing logic of neoliberalism. If this is true, however, it suggests that just as much as the content of right-wing pseudopoliticization—what it opposes and what it aims at—needs to be taken into account, its form must be taken into account as well in order to arrive at not only an adequate analysis but also a more complex sense of what shape a response to it from the Left should take.

2. "LEFT POPULISM" AND THE PROBLEM OF POLITICAL FORM

Brown's analysis of the affective basis and dynamic of right-wing authoritarianism adds an important layer of complexity to common invocations of anger or a sense of abandonment and desperation in attempts
to explain what has gone wrong. Especially in the discussion about the
need for, and prospects of, a left populism,[17] it often seems as if the affective basis of the authoritarian Right could just as well be the affective
basis of a leftist, emancipatory political project. (If only Sanders had
faced Trump, the narrative suggests, most Trump voters would have
voted for Sanders, but with Clinton as the alternative they were left with
no choice. Similar stories are told about how those voting for Le Pen
could only be reached by Mélenchon's embrace of national identity. All
these stories are characterized by a rather speculative political sociology and an obfuscation of political responsibility.)

In foregrounding the question "What is the political form of this
anger and its mobilization?,"[18] my sense is that Brown opens up the
space for a response to the authoritarian backlash that neither falls into
the neoliberal trap of depoliticization nor advocates what I take to be a
left populism that is simplistic both in its analysis—a "hydraulic" model
of society in which affective pressures that are simmering under the surface of liberal democracies get agitated by third-way postpolitics and
can then be tapped into by either the Right or the Left and mobilized
for a reactionary or an emancipatory project, respectively[19]—and in its
understanding of what kind of politics this analysis calls for.

In a first step, it seems crucial to call attention to the different types
of affect at play here: their differing social and experiential bases, political valences, and political dynamics (and their potential to be enlisted
in a dynamic of politicization or to drag us back into the traps of pseudopoliticization). With Brown and Fassin[20] and against Chantal Mouffe
it can be argued that ressentiment, rancor, rage, a desire for revenge
experienced by the historically dominant, and their sense of "aggrieved
power" in the face of "lost entitlement" are not the same—do not have
the same bases and do not follow the same political logic or allow for the
same political mobilization—as anger and outrage at unjust and undemocratic forms of exploitation, exclusion, and domination experienced by

historically disadvantaged groups. To be sure, there is no sharp and stable distinction between regressive and emancipatory affects, and of course justified anger and outrage can also turn destructive and even disempowering; but this complexity of the political logic of affect should not overshadow the important difference that, on many levels, including that of political affect, acting out of a "sense of abandonment" is not equivalent to responding to abandonment, and struggling to maintain exclusion and domination is not equivalent to struggling for inclusion and emancipation.

In fact, this is a point Theodor W. Adorno already highlighted in a 1967 talk on right-wing radicalism: not actual but anticipated, imagined, feared abandonment, a sensed loss of privileges one has come to see as natural, is the driving force of this reactionary anti-politics.[21] It is not just, or even primarily, the worst off who are voting for Trump, Le Pen, and the German far-right Alternative für Deutschland (AfD), and the storming of the US Capitol was not a revolt of the oppressed and exploited but of mostly middle-class and in many cases middle-aged white people who spontaneously joined several well-organized militia. This is not to say that there are no actual problems—such as deindustrialization, the opioid epidemic, and a growing split between rural and urban lifeworlds—that might drive people to turn to right-wing authoritarianism, or that they have no legitimate grievances whatsoever, especially in a political constellation where the Left has indeed failed to effectively address the destruction wrought by neoliberalism. But the standard story, according to which right-wing populism and the new authoritarianism are best understood and explained as the class revenge of those who have been left behind by globalization and no longer feel at home in their own country, is both bad social science and legitimating ideology, resting on a double confusion between the relative loss of privilege and actual decline, and between a (political and analytical) return to class and a return to the white working class.[22]

There is another relevant feature of the new authoritarian Right that Adorno identified and that drives a wedge into the presumably unified phenomenon of populism: the adherents of right-wing populism do not attribute the blame for the abandonment they experience and anticipate to the structural logic of society; rather, they personalize it and project it onto groups they classify as alien and not belonging. This is why the fundamental structure of right-wing populism (or better: authoritarianism) is not dyadic as is claimed in analyses that see the shared structure of right- and left-wing populism in opposing the people to the elite. Rather, its structure is triadic, turning the "true people" against the elite *and* against those minorities—today migrants and Muslims in particular— that are seen as infiltrating society, being "coddled" by the establishment, and taking away from the "true people" what is rightfully theirs.[23]

149

However catchy the talk of a populist moment, of the moment of populism—as the political strategy of the symbolic invocation and activation of the "real," "true," or "authentic people"—might be, it therefore conceals significant differences between the political movements categorized under this label. They neither react to the same problem nor are they grounded in or mobilize the same motivations and affects. They do not share the same goals, and they do not exhibit the same political form. It is simply not the case that—as the idea of a "populist moment" suggests—movements that are often characterized as right-wing populist—such as the AfD in Germany, the Trump campaign, or the Dutch Forum for Democracy—can usefully be grouped together with what are sometimes characterized as left-wing populist movements such as Occupy, Podemos, or Syriza. Just pointing to a shared mistrust toward institutions and other forms of mediation and representation, as well as to the desire for participation and "presentism" by those alienated from traditional representative politics, and then ascribing a shared logic of politicization to these movements—as authors inspired by the work of Pierre Rosanvallon tend to do to[24]—is neither empirically nor theoretically and certainly not politically convincing.

Even if we abstract from the declared aims of most of the right-wing movements and parties of today that are hard to categorize as democratic or democratizing, given that they often explicitly aim at excluding racialized subsets of the population and even of the citizenry from the political community, their antidemocratic and ultimately antipolitical character is mirrored in their political form. It is expressed in and informs the way in which they are internally structured (e.g., in hierarchical and vertical rather than horizontal ways, etc.), how they either enable or suppress and curtail dissent, reflexivity, and self-critique, and what kinds of strategies of immunization and regressive forms of identity formation they allow for.

In this context, two theoretical moves that we find in Brown's recent work seem especially promising. The first consists in a return to early Frankfurt School attempts to theorize the form of fascist and neofascist politics. I would add two aspects to Brown's focus on Herbert Marcuse's notion of "repressive desublimation"—that is, a form of desublimation that involves a "daring and disinhibition (manifest today in Alt-Right tweets, blogs, trolling, and public conduct) [that] symptomizes or iterates, rather than counters the order's violence and prejudices, as well as its ordinary values."[25] With Adorno we can get a better sense of the "malicious, repressive egalitarianism" of right-wing populism that is structured by an all-pervasive "rigid distinction between the beloved in-group and the rejected out-group,"[26] taking into account the fusion between nonliberatory transgression and oppressive submission Marcuse tried to capture.[27] And with Leo Löwenthal[28] we can see that the "false prophets" of the authoritarian Right resemble quack doctors whose misdiagnosis only leads to pseudosolutions that prevent the problem—actual, potential, anticipated, perceived, or imaginary economic deprivation and "dethronement"—from being adequately framed, let alone addressed, displacing it onto another terrain—prominently that of anti-migrant and anti-refugee discourse and policy—and leading to the replacement of politics by irrational outbursts.[29]

The second move that can be found in the ambivalent epilogue to *Undoing the Demos* is a return to Occupy and the politics of the assembly. What remains from this political moment that now seems so far away?[30] Apart from the lasting achievement of having forced "the grammar of the social, including its importance to democracy" back into public discourse,[31] the Left inherits from Occupy an awareness that, given the history of political struggle and organization on the left, it is always a good (and today a particularly urgent) question to ask: "And might we also need to examine the ways these logics and energies organize aspects of left responses to contemporary predicaments?"[32] This question is always pertinent, as there is no guarantee that ties the emancipatory "content" of movements to the "right form."

As I read them, the emphasis on horizontal, pluralist, and inclusive (vs. vertical, hierarchical, and uniformity-oriented) structures of organization (not just ideologies) and self-reflection within the movements of the squares, such as Occupy, the Gezi Park protests in Istanbul, and the Spanish anti-austerity movement 15-M, were aimed precisely at keeping that question present against the pressures of hegemonic or populist politics that privilege politico-aesthetic formations built around imagined and artificially produced homogeneity, determinacy, and the absence of ambiguity (that are then imagined as naturally given and prepolitical). Indeed, we can see these very commitments centrally at work in the movements of the squares, as they recognized and tried to mirror them in their practice of assembling and in their discourse that not only rejected the established politics of "us vs. them"—prominently in the refusal of hegemonic discourses of othering (ötekileştirme) in Gezi Park—but informed a radical expansion of the repertoire of contestation and of organization in a prefigurative key.[33]

Against this background, both neoliberalism and right-wing authoritarianism can be seen as attacks on the uniquely political project of democratic power-sharing within a demos or among *demoi*, characterized by irreducible plurality and heterogeneity. But if this pluralist understanding of the political should be at the core of any Left response to both neoliberalism and right-wing authoritarianism, what could an alternative form of remaking the demos under such conditions look like? What should caution us against an all too easy embrace of the idea of a left populism is the readily observable tendency of officially anti-essentialist invocations of the "true people" (and presumably that means ones that are attentive to the exclusions and marginalizations produced by these invocations) to succumb to, and indeed contribute to the escalation of, an essentializing and exclusionary dynamic. Actually existing "left populism" offers plenty of examples, from the flag-waving La France Insoumise to the Italian anti-immigration and Salvini-enabling Cinque Stelle to the German movement Aufstehen, whose proponents—presumably leftist politicians such as Sarah Wagenknecht and Oskar Lafontaine, but also their intellectual sympathizers such as Wolfgang Streeck—do not shy away from advocating nationalism, as well as mimicking and thereby endorsing and normalizing right-wing anti-immigrant rhetoric. In all these cases, the populist recoding of presumably leftist political orientations drives out whatever emancipatory potential these movements might have been able to claim in the past. The deeper reason for this dynamic can be seen in what Nicholas de Genova characterizes as the deep nationalist logic of populist appeals to the "real people" in an "us vs. them" register: "All manifestations of populism serve to recapture the insurgent energies of emancipatory struggles and entrap the 'common folk' within the borders of the Nation, reinscribing a democratic political enclosure whereby human life is subordinated to and subjected by the nationalist metaphysics of state power."[34]

3. REMAKING *DEMOI* FROM BELOW

In a more theoretical vein, the question could then be formulated as follows: If there is a political need to acknowledge and institutionalize as far as possible "the open and contestable signification of democracy" and find ways to "release democracy from containment by any particular form while insisting on its value in connoting political self-rule by the people, whoever the people are,"[35] within the forms of organization and self-understanding of democratic struggles and movements, and if these commitments can therefore not just be commitments the theorist holds but does not expect to be upheld in practice, what are the consequences for thinking about emancipatory politics in the register of hegemony, populism, and hegemonic populism? My claim is that struggles for emancipation "from the left" cannot have the same form and follow the same logic as struggles for hegemony "from the right," which are evidently not concerned with, and indeed embrace the task of, constructing an exclusionary and homogeneous collective subject that can serve as the firm ground of affective identification and mobilization. Against this background, the need for internal reflexivity or other ways of keeping the deep plurality and heterogeneity of political subject positions and lines of conflict open is more than a strategic disadvantage for the Left.

Maybe we can find cues for an alternative way of undoing the demos and remaking *demoi* from forms of political struggle that question established notions of "the people" and its boundaries but that might not end up embracing a positive vision of "We, the People" in the singular. Does their struggle follow the same logic of hegemonic claim-making? Surely there are limits to any abstract discussion of this question, but let me, in closing, briefly indicate some reasons for doubting that the answer could be a simple yes.

153

The struggles and movements I have in mind center on contesting existing configurations of the political community and claim the need for its reconfiguration from below or from the margins. The practices and theories generated in these struggles point to ways in which the processual, conflictual, and open-ended character of politics can be defended against the temptations of closure and hierarchical reinscription into the homogenizing logic of hegemony that the populist model advocates. In the contemporary constellation, these are primarily migrant and Indigenous struggles and movements. Without pretending that these heterogeneous struggles are unified by a common goal or a shared organizational form, they can be seen as standing in the tradition of struggles highlighting that it is often precisely those who do not count as citizens, or even as political agents—enslaved people, women, workers, colonized subjects, migrants, refugees, Indigenous peoples—who develop new, or rearticulate preexisting, forms of citizenship and democracy that promise to be more adequate to our current political constellation of disaggregated sovereignty, traversed as it is by transnational challenges, power relations, actors, and struggles.

In a settler-colonial context, struggles for self-determination by Indigenous and occupied people and peoples clash with the state's claim to exclusive territorial sovereignty.[36] The radically democratic potential of Indigenous struggles today can be seen precisely in the dual displacement of hegemony, which can no longer serve as the privileged logic of political articulation, and of the modern nation-state, which can no longer serve as the unquestioned terrain for democratic struggle.[37] As a result, Indigenous struggles for self-determination and against the colonial and imperial project of the modern nation-state to

impose homogeneity and (territorial, cultural, political, legal) uniformity escape both the framework of protest and that of dominant notions
of civility, even if they might appear as "constituent powers" and "civic
powers" in the plural.[38] At the same time, they fundamentally transform
the very meaning of "self-determination" beyond the bounded and sovereign model of the (individual or collective) self toward an acknowl-
edgment of the interdependency and relationality of all (human and
nonhuman) members of the community.

Similarly, and despite important differences, in a world in which
nation-states claim a unilateral right to control their borders—both the
borders of their territory and the borders of membership and belonging—migrant and refugee movements challenge a whole way of life and
a political imaginary that entirely abstracts from its own structural
implication in the production of the conditions that violate migrants'
"right to stay" as well as their "right to escape."[39]

These struggles—which are, of course, also struggles for and over
politicization and the boundaries of the political and which do not
engage in the abstract celebration of plural subject positions for its own
sake—seem to be misidentified both in their content and in their form
when they are interpreted as contestatory responses to the question of
"who the people really are." The "We" in "We didn't cross the border,
the border crossed us" and "We are here because you were/are there" is
not, and does not aspire to be, the same as the "We" in "We, the People." Not all political and social struggles of our age can be articulated
equally well, if at all, in the language of popular sovereignty, of sovereignty, and of the people in the singular. At the very least, they seem to
require a radical revision, pluralization, and deterritorialization of the
demos, of peoplehood and of its internal and external borders—all in
ways that deeply unsettle the existing terms of the struggle for hegemony rather than making a move within its narrowly national-populist
confines. Such nationalist-populist articulations would also miss the
prefigurative potential that resides in the ways in which these struggles challenge and transcend the dominant logic of the nation-state and
its border regime by developing, resuscitating, and enacting alternative
forms of political agency, belonging, and solidarity in the here and now.
In this context, the point is not to find a new vanguard in Indigenous

and migrant struggles onto which frustrated revolutionary desires can be projected, but to see the collective enactment of denied freedoms, the temporary realization of utopian possibilities in the here and now, and the practical de-centering of the state for what they are: openings of political space that reveal a radical-democratic potential. The question is, which practices and forms of organization can accommodate rather than repress and conceal *this* political potential that seems to push beyond hegemony?

155

NOTES

1. For some influential examples, from radically different theoretical vantage points, see Jacques Rancière, *Disagreement* (Minneapolis: University of Minnesota Press, 1999 [1995]); Colin Crouch, *Post-democracy* (Cambridge, UK: Polity, 2004); Chantal Mouffe, *On the Political* (London: Routledge, 2005).
2. See, e.g., Jürgen Habermas, *Theory and Practice* (Boston: Beacon Press, 1973 [1963]).
3. See also Wendy Brown, *In the Ruins of Neoliberalism: The Rise of Antidemocratic Politics in the West* (New York: Columbia University Press, 2019), 28.
4. The political sociology and comparative politics literature is full of titles, including variations of the phrase "the politicization of migration."
5. Wendy Brown, Peter E. Gordon, and Max Pensky, "Introduction: Critical Theory in an Authoritarian Age," in *Authoritarianism: Three Inquiries in Critical Theory* (Chicago: University of Chicago Press, 2018), 1.
6. Wendy Brown, "Neoliberalism's Frankenstein: Authoritarian Freedom in Twenty-First Century 'Democracies,'" in ibid., 11.
7. Brown, *In the Ruins of Neoliberalism*, 108–9, 117–18.
8. Colin Crouch, "Post-democracy and Populism," *Political Quarterly* 90 (2019): 124–37, esp. 129 and 135.
9. Wendy Brown, "'Society Must Be Dismantled': Markets, Morals, and Freedom," Gauss Lecture, Princeton University, October 2, 2018.
10. Brown, *In the Ruins of Neoliberalism*, 60, 95, 115, 118.
11. Brown, Gordon, and Pensky, "Introduction," 3.
12. Brown, "Neoliberalism's Frankenstein," 8–9. See also Brown, *In the Ruins of Neoliberalism*, 2.
13. Brown, *In the Ruins of Neoliberalism*, 57.
14. Brown, "Neoliberalism's Frankenstein," 34. See also Brown, *In the Ruins of Neoliberalism*, 85.
15. See Brown, *In the Ruins of Neoliberalism*, 56–57, 199n3.
16. Brown, "Neoliberalism's Frankenstein," 36. See also Brown, *In the Ruins of Neoliberalism*, 178.
17. I do not here consider the question of left populism in South America, where it is part of an entirely different political constellation.

18. Brown, "Neoliberalism's Frankenstein," 10.
19. This model is famously advanced by Chantal Mouffe, e.g., in *On the Political* and more recently in *For a Left Populism* (London: Verso, 2018).
20. See Èric Fassin, *Populisme: Le grand ressentiment* (Paris: Textuel, 2017).
21. Theodor W. Adorno, *Aspekte des neuen Rechtsradikalismus* (Berlin: Suhrkamp, 2019).
22. See Gurminder K. Bhambra, "Brexit, Trump, and 'Methodological Whiteness': On the Misrecognition of Race and Class," *British Journal of Sociology* 68 (2017): 214–32.
23. See also John Judis, "Us v Them: The Birth of Populism," *The Guardian*, October 13, 2016, https://www.theguardian.com/politics/2016/oct/13/birth-of-popu lism-donald-trump.
24. See Pierre Rosanvallon, *Counter-Democracy: Politics in an Age of Distrust* (Cambridge: Cambridge University Press, 2008 [2006]), chap. 12, "The Populist Temptation."
25. Brown, *In the Ruins of Neoliberalism*, 167.
26. Especially Theodor W. Adorno, "Freudian Theory and the Pattern of Fascist Propaganda," in *Gesammelte Schriften*, vol. 8 (Frankfurt am Main: Suhrkamp, 1972 [1951]), 408–33.
27. See Brown, *In the Ruins of Neoliberalism*, 165–70.
28. See, in particular, Leo Löwenthal and Norbert Guterman, "Portrait of the American Agitator," *Public Opinion Quarterly* 12, no. 3 (1948): 417–29.
29. As Löwenthal and Guterman write (ibid., 426): "Under the guise of a protest against the oppressive situation, the agitator binds his audience to it. Since this pseudo-protest never produces a genuine solution, it merely leads the audience to seek permanent relief from a permanent predicament by means of irrational outbursts."
30. See Wendy Brown, *Undoing the Demos: Neoliberalism's Stealth Revolution* (New York: Zone Books, 2015), epilogue; and Robin Celikates and Yolande Jansen, "Reclaiming Democracy: An Interview with Wendy Brown on Occupy, Sovereignty, and Secularism," *Krisis* (2012/13): 68–77.
31. Brown, *In the Ruins of Neoliberalism*, 53.
32. Brown, "Neoliberalism's Frankenstein," 36.
33. See, e.g., Robin Celikates, "Learning from the Streets: Civil Disobedience in Theory and Practice," in *Global Activism: Art and Conflict in the 21st Century*, ed. Peter Weibel (Cambridge: MIT Press, 2015), 65–72.
34. Nicholas de Genova, "Rebordering 'the People': Notes on Theorizing Populism," *South Atlantic Quarterly* 117, no. 2 (2018): 368.
35. Brown, *Undoing the Demos*, 20.
36. See, e.g., Audra Simpson, *Mohawk Interruptus: Political Life Across the Borders of Settler States* (Durham: Duke University Press, 2014).
37. See Janet Conway and Jakeet Singh, "Radical Democracy in Global Perspective: Notes from the Pluriverse," *Third World Quarterly* 32, no. 4 (2011): 689–706.
38. See James Tully, *Public Philosophy in a New Key*, vol. 2: *Imperialism and Civic Freedom* (Cambridge: Cambridge University Press, 2009), 195–221, 243–309.
39. See, e.g., Robin Celikates, "Constituent Power Beyond Exceptionalism: Irregular Migration, Disobedience, and (Re-)Constitution," *Journal of Interna-

tional Political Theory 15, no. 1 (2019): 67–81; Sandro Mezzadra, *Diritto di fuga* (Verona: Ombre Corte, 2006). For a response to the claim that Indigenous commitments to land and jurisdiction betray an antimigrant and anti-Black character, see Glen Sean Coulthard, "Response," *Historical Materialism* 24, no. 3 (2016): 96.

CHAPTER 9

Thinking Together

Reply to Critics

Wendy Brown

The time, labor, erudition, imagination, and generosity in these essays are extraordinary gifts from fellow thinkers. Reading them left me both surprised and instructed, only occasionally flinching. I was surprised by their revelation of certain lines of generativity and intellectual coherence across four decades of work that I had experienced more as accidents of intellectual influence and interest, and reactions to immediate political forces and events. I was instructed by compelling critiques of my blind spots, limiting allergies and attachments, troubling omissions, and neglected interlocutions.

Above all, I am grateful for the fierce and overt politicalness of these essays. My own original attraction to political theory, and formation within it, assumed its ambition to illuminate the predicaments and potentials arising from the powers organizing common dimensions of human existence.[1] Since those naïve beginnings, I have struggled to sustain the worldliness of political theory against its unworlding by contemporary norms of professionalization, especially those of severe historicism, on the one hand, and ahistorical analytic abstraction, on the other. This struggle has generally required abandoning political theory's main streams and engaging with and across other disciplines and literatures.[2] It is enormously heartening that the scholars in this volume are also bound to the worlding of political theory. Each argues for the epistemologies, cosmologies, thematics, or categories of analysis that they believe refract our common existence and predicaments, through theorizing, for example, depoliticization, hyperpoliticization, and the very nature of politics; figures of feminism and modes of social reproduction; temporalities of power and the powers of temporality; the limits of the concept of political imaginaries or formulations of political desublimation.

159

The following reflections work orthogonally to the provocations of these essays. My aim is to sketch a cluster of contemporary left political theoretical conundrums: problems in the world that are problematics for theory but novel enough that political-theoretical frames and categories have not caught up to them. These problematics might be termed the politics of emergency, the venue of democracy in a globalized order, and a post-truth civil war. I only make the case for each problematic, without actually developing them in ways that would contribute to what Stuart Hall, following Gramsci, termed our current conjuncture.

These considerations involve revisiting some themes that have long occupied me, but in order to rethink them rather than repeat myself. I am generally more inclined to rethinking and revising than defending or extending previous arguments. Of course, I have certain enduring concerns, with the varieties of subjugating and undemocratic power, with historiography and genealogy, with capitalism, liberalism, sovereignty, and wounded masculinity. Liberalism's cruelties and dissimulations are perennial bugbears for me, and I have forever resisted the colonization of democracy's promise by both liberalism and capitalism. I have always approached left critique and left justice projects somewhat askance from the main intellectual traditions forming both, allowing Nietzsche, Weber, Freud, Schmitt, and Foucault to clang around with the Marx, Rousseau, Fanon, Stuart Hall, and feminist and critical race theorists in my head. And within the Frankfurt School that loosely knits us together here, I find more inspiration in the spurned Marcuse than the valorized Adorno and in the early rather than the late Habermas. In all of this, as Eduardo Mendieta suggests, freedom has been my lodestar. However, this lodestar, as my own essay in this volume makes clear, is one about whose coordinates and content I remain uncertain, even uneasy.

Apart from these constants, my objects change, my worries and angles of inquiry change, and hopefully my thinking changes as the times require and I am persuaded of earlier elisions and intellectual missteps. Like many, I have been humbled in recent years both by my lifelong failures to adequately feature racial supremacy on the landscape of undemocratic powers in the euro-atlantic world, and to take the measure of planetary finitude as an objective problem and one "altering the aspect" of every political concept.[3] I do not especially value intellectual consistency and am slightly repelled by political, social, or cultural theorists for whom it is a measure of anything, especially insight or profundity. I prefer examining tensions to making tight arguments and pursuing new questions thrown up by the world to solving what the trade now calls "puzzles" drawn from the discipline. I do not believe thinking ever overcomes its historical and social predicates, that we can depart ourselves, even as Nietzsche and Foucault remind us that the most powerful thought not only disrupts the coordinates of the present but also undoes the thinker.[4] I am suspicious of thinking that does not try to avow its investments or what spurs it. I have never been crypto-normative, only open-handedly normative.

Thus, Johanna Oksala is right to see tensions in my approach to the political, but I wonder if resolution rather than consideration of their ground is the most fecund move with these tensions. Robyn Marasco is right to see feminism everywhere in my work and is generous to identify my changing views with "maturity"; however, that term may obscure deeper oscillations and ambivalences in my relationship to feminist theory. Sometimes I am reworking it from within, other times wielding it against a masculinist order of things it did not know was there, and still other times attacking its narrowness or blinders. While I know that feminism is indispensable to my survival and sanity, as well as that of the world, I have also always feared entrapment by it, including and perhaps especially by its niche in political theory. (Denise Riley has captured this fear splendidly: "Can anyone fully inhabit a gender without a degree of horror . . . make a final home in that classification without suffering claustrophobia?").[5] Loren Goldman calls out my relentless tendencies toward historical synchronicity and (hence) social totality when non-synchronicity might better serve my critique of progressive narratives and seed more possible struggles for better futures. Still, I am suspicious of happy metaphysics and convenient historiographies—whether in the Deleuzians or in that paradoxically grim theorist of hope, Ernst Bloch. And I myself am not hopeful, although I believe it is our secular human obligation to create hope in and for our woeful world. Eduardo Mendieta is right to worry about defoundationalizing all left analyses and norms and about genealogical critiques that disrupt the present without settling upon or even suggesting the political entailment of that disruption. Asad Haider spies danger and disingenuousness in adapting the neo-essentialism of Freud and Marcuse in order to grasp the disinhibitions of the contemporary political: How can we talk about desublimation of instinctual energies in a poststructuralist subject? Yes, but if we do not find a way to incorporate nihilistic desublimation into our understanding of right-wing rage, we will always find ourselves back at the tired and limited questions of whether it is the wounded status of their class, race, or gender that animates the contemporary ethnonationalist Right. In insisting on thinking about *demoi* that could emerge between modalities of depoliticization and hyperpoliticization today, Robin Celikates goes to the heart of the contemporary problematic for twenty-first-century democratic theory and practice: What are the prospects of deep pluralization and spatial unboundedness when democracy has only ever been approximated through homogeneity and borders? Is this approximation revealing of democracy's "truth" or only the historical limitation imposed on it by its (Western) civilizational birthplace and modern imbrication with Westphalian nation-states, colonialism, and liberalism? Does democracy require supplements or deep transformation in this regard?

So much for preliminaries. Time to go in. There are two striking things about the subject orientation of politically alert working- and middle-class millennials and older Gen Z-ers. First, given the accelerating pace and effects of climate change, they have no confidence that the planet will remain livable or even last through what is supposed to be their lifetime. Second, socioeconomically, they know they don't have a shot at what their parents and grandparents had—debt-free education leading to relative job security or easeful career trajectories, affordable housing however modest, the resources and stability to raise children, a comfortable retirement. Instead, they must try to make something of themselves through entrepreneurial, self-investing, and self-promotional strategies large and small, in a world where unpaid internships, a limited social state, unaffordable health care, and gig or contract jobs without benefits have become the norm.

Consequently, on the one hand, they feel existential terror or extreme fatalism or futility; on the other hand, they feel an imperative to dedicate every waking hour to plotting their individual course through social, economic, and technological orders changing by the nanosecond, changes they are required to anticipate and navigate just in order to survive, let alone thrive. In what many of their parents and grandparents experienced (depending on class and cultural positions, of course) as the relatively carefree years of their teens and twenties, they are frantically trying to curate and secure futures for themselves in what they understand to be end-times.

Most recognize the social schizophrenia of this condition. Psychically, it adds up to long-run fatalism, even nihilistic despair, combined with short-run anxiety that is unappeasable, sometimes crippling. Indeed, depression and anxiety, along with drugs and "wellness" regimens prescribed for both, have become ordinary rather than deviant states for this generation. Politically, this condition is the context for their wariness, if not outright hostility, toward both capitalism and parliamentary democracy, the one for its failure to sustain either species life or their individual prospects, the other for its apparent indifference to and incapacity to stem this failure. They are alert to capitalism's pace of deracinating if not destroying everything alive, to the dinosaur qualities of the political systems it outfoxes, and to the relative complacency of their elders who enjoyed the last decent era with both. March for Our Lives, Sunrise Movement, Extinction Rebellion, Black Lives Matter—these represent the organized political manifestations of this consciousness in the United States. Perhaps nothing captures it better, however, than the viral blowback to the 2019 confrontation between a finger-wagging Diane Feinstein and a group of politically urgent youngsters whom she demanded defer to her decades of political experience dealing with climate change, as if those decades established credibility rather than abject failure.[6] The organized defeat of a groundswell on the left by the Democratic National Committee in 2020 also underlines the millennial / Gen Z sense that their elders care more about their own home values, low taxes, and 401(k)s than the future, or even racial justice or school shootings. Above all, they feel alone but righteous in their recognition that the capitalist game—of dependence on endless growth, financial speculation, gross inequality, and fossil fuels—is up.

In addition to depression, fatalism, and survivalism, what emerges from this generation is a politics of emergency. In their organized bids to save the very possibility of individual and collective futurity (Extinction Rebellion, Sunrise Movement), social justice (BLM, #MeToo, Ni Una Menos), or security from violence (March for Our Lives), they are unmoved by the interest group pluralism, labyrinthine laws, procedures, or power-sharing, let alone plutocratic corruption, of constitutional democracy today. They are underwhelmed by tired debates about regulated versus unregulated markets, or a politics of freedom versus a politics of redistribution in thinking about capitalism. They spurn neo-Weberian accounts of political change as a "slow boring of hard boards" centered on the state or state-like institutions. Nor, however, does this politics of emergency comport with the Hegelian Marxist tradition of revolution born from the historical ripening of conditions for *Aufhebung.* It rejects not only a historiography but a *politics* of progress (as does its reactionary sibling, right-wing authoritarian populism, but that is a matter for another essay). Closer to Benjamin's "activation of the emergency brake" on the runaway train of history, it calls for radical rupture in the name of justice and survival and seeks a mass will to enact that rupture. The stakes are so high that this politics of emergency is not afraid of losing what it has, which is the fear that ordinarily keeps rupture politics in check.[7] For this generation, hegemonic political and economic norms and forms brought us to this pass, and they will not carry us through it.

Rejecting European modernity's progressivism and its self-anointment as the zenith of civilizational maturity, this politics of emergency represents far more than the impatience of youth or the particular existential threat of the climate crisis. It may also signal the beginnings of working through nihilism, progressivism's theological twin. Nihilism in the West arises when value systems are degrounded by science and reason and are therefore severely weakened without being surrendered or replaced. Nihilism thus understood is not an individual attitude, nor is it a universal form. Rather, it is a specific historical condition emanating from the specific trajectory of Western theism and European modernity. The features and entailments of this condition are many; the two most relevant to this discussion are the limited faith in and low esteem for the species that nihilism spawns, together with the deep disorientation it also generates before the task of generating postfoundational values. Working through nihilism requires mourning one kind of meaning and value generation and arriving at another, especially in finding new sources for governing values. It requires accepting that humans alone generate value; that value is made, not discovered; and that accepting the burden of this work together is inescapable.

Nietzsche knew that such a working-through was all that could redeem humanity if that redemption was not deferred to the figure of the *Übermensch*—a figure hard to treat seriously as capable of overcoming nihilism, of shouldering the work of crafting our individual and collective selves after the gods are gone. Working through nihilism must aim at affirming humanity—its worth, capacities, powers—at the ends of histories founded in gods, culminating in their destruction, and leaving only disenchantment, trivia, or cheapness in its wake. Working through nihilism involves taking responsibility for creating values after the value-apocalypse emanating from the specific sequence of Christianity, reason, philosophy, and science. Ethically and politically, working through nihilism entails developing shared criteria for deciding rather than deriving (from an imagined table of values fixed in stone) how we should live on the earth and with one another. It requires creating and instantiating value after the collapse of systems that "looked outside the world" for moral direction and sources of power to direct our fates. It requires deciding what to live for and how we should live together, by what ordering principles and paradigms. In this regard, working through nihilism is a foundation for building a democracy *not* "under God."

If I am right that Gen Z and millennial left politics may be understood as working through nihilism, as becoming postnihilist, the politics of emergency gives this work a special cast unanticipated by the classical theorists of nihilism—Nietzsche, Tolstoy, Dostoyevsky, Weber, and Heidegger. Because there is a planet to rescue from immediate danger, not only values to create, the work requires concentrated attention to becoming responsible for human powers and to organizing them sustainably, *yesterday*. This is the deep meaning of an emergency postprogressive, postnihilist politics. Dialectics, contradictions, horizontalism, pragmatism—none of these can help us here.

At the same time, postnihilists cannot do this work out of whole cloth. How often we "freethinkers" must remind ourselves that a new world is not born from new concepts, that we cannot invent let alone impose de novo forms of governing reason, economy, or polity; that (to shift into a Foucauldian register) we always think, work, and craft ourselves and society from relations of immanence, even when we believe ourselves to be in radical rebellion. Yet how to square this limitation with a politics of emergency? How to wrestle with historically imposed constraints on the thinkable and the possible when we are at the edge of a crumbling cliff? How to break with old humanist conceits saturating political vocabularies and institutions while also tapping the maturity to reject political projects that advocate clean breaks or historical overleaps? This is the predicament posed by the climate crisis and of forms of political economy and ways of life that would be responsive to it. It is possible that Goldman's asynchronous temporalities could be helpful here, but it may also be that asynchrony and deep social differentiation and dis-integration compound the difficulties of comprehending and meeting this state of emergency.[8] Don't we need all hands on deck, and for all to be on one deck, facing the storm? Isn't this the truth that our contemporary Cassandra, Greta Thunberg, cries out? If so, unprecedented ontological and epistemological shifts, and not only political and economic ones, are required for our particular postnihilist politics.

We will return to this conundrum of historical possibilities and temporalities in the face of the climate emergency near the end of this chapter. I want to turn now to several other novel features of our times that present special challenges to political theory today.

It is widely recognized that we are in a protracted interregnum of political forms. Both the nation-state and the parliamentary democracy designed to govern and legitimate it are nearly exhausted. Yet the nation-state remains such a passionate object of belonging and fealty, as well as a venue of economic and political management, that the floods of capital, goods, humans, cultures, finance, and technology challenging its integrity and boundedness are met by a ferocious counterforce: border guards and fortifications, xenophobic and ethnonationalist politics and policies, demagogic politicians defending its might and right, and quotidian nationalisms, including on the left. Parliamentary democracy strikes many as the only stable port in the twenty-first-century political storms. "It's true that the parliamentary systems in most of our countries have become ossified and their democratic potentialities are minimal," Étienne Balibar remarks, "but the elimination of every notion of representation might be a very dangerous gamble, at least for the time being."[9]

Like the exhausting and exhausted capitalist order bringing the planet and its inhabitants to the brink, this political interregnum is a condition to be reckoned with, not simply criticized. It frames the problematic with which Robin Celikates concludes his chapter: What or who is the demos that would challenge antidemocratic powers today, whether those of finance, of extractive or hyperexploitative capitalism, or of authoritarian, patriarchal ethnonationalism? What designates or demarcates "the people" of a postnational, postcolonial, postracial, and postpatriarchal democratic formation? If we reject the nationalist Left of Wolfgang Streeck or Bernie Sanders, then where exactly does democracy take shape?[10] If we quickly say "beyond the nation-state" or "globally," besides being vague, are we sure? The Left fiercely criticized the EU Troika's 2015 trammeling of Greek sovereignty with neoliberal austerity measures, those long practiced by the IMF on debtor nations in the Global South to which we also objected. We decry America's long history of trampling Central and South American democracies, along with Russian interference in American electoral politics. We support sovereign statehood for Palestine, for the Kurds, for Puerto Rico. In short, we ferociously defend nation-state democracy and sovereignty when settler colonialism, empire, the Troika, big banks, big tech, or Russian trolls threaten, deny, or subvert them. Yet we engage in transnational solidarities to protest certain state actions or decrees that may emerge from legitimately elected representatives. This oscillation is itself an expression of interregnum consciousness.

Other questions pop out of the Pandora's box of the interregnum. Why defend democracy at all in the twenty-first century?[11] What does it offer to the multifaceted globalization of life today and to our neglected kinship with other species and even nonsentient life as one of Western civilization's most consequential failures? Why cleave to democracy and to what I have insisted is its essential predicate, a robust appreciation of distinctly political powers and capacities? Here I am especially addressing Johanna Oksala's suspicion about an old-white-boy history of political thought hangover in my thinking when it comes to the political and her own preference for affirming "resistance and solidarity against neoliberalism" that "bring[s] together many kinds of seemingly separate struggles."[12]

Resistance, which has often transmogrified from tactic to end amid the post-Marxist waning of revolutionary horizons, should not be confused with ruling ourselves, the promise of democracy. Vital as a practice, resistance challenges existing regimes and technologies of subjection or exploitation. Solidarity with others is its prime power, as it converts individual or small-group rebellion into a force for change. Resistance, solidarity, and even social change, however, are different from the project of building a democratic regime, which depends upon sharing equally in powers of rule, including with those whom one does not necessarily have solidarity.[13] Of course, there are threads of connection between resistance and the aspiration to democratic rule; left prefigurative politics and horizontalism today aim to articulate these threads. But one index of the crisis of progress—not in the intellectual register that Loren Goldman offers in his elegant corrective of my reading of the moderns, but in the lived, hard stop to illusions of progressive history among left and right activists—is precisely that resistance is often tacitly figured as an end or good in itself. This is so for a range of movements against state violence of all kinds, racialized policing and incarceration, male supremacy, and the molten hot powers of finance. And it is certainly so for much of the political activity of the anarchist Left. Thus, in some ways it is not surprising that in place of my argument for building radical democracy, Oksala calls for a "militant queer feminist political front against neoliberalism . . . confronting and pushing against the male dominated left."[14] The question, however, is: How does this political front transmute into taking power and embodying rule? How does it exceed resistance and solidarity to become a democratic regime shaping common life? If this question seems foreign or impertinent, that may be a measure of left fatalism or despair.

As resistance is substituted for rule, the hardest questions of democratizing power today—with whom, with what means, over what powers, dealing with what differences, and above all, entailing what boundaries or exclusions—go by the wayside. Ruling ourselves is never complete, of course; there is a persistent partiality and incompleteness to democratizing power. Like freedom, democracy is an ongoing project, not a final achievement or possession, especially because of the challenge of sharing rule over all the powers that govern us. Even if we collectively owned and controlled production, technology, and finance; even if we abolished the powers, privileges, and affects of whiteness and (cis)heteronormativity; even if we ended masculinist control over reproduction and female sexuality, and masculinist dominance in the public sphere, remaining would be all the other powers Foucault and Freud identified as regulating aspects of being together that are relatively untouched by these revolutionary aspirations. Collectivizing control of all the powers making and organizing us is impossible, even if we broaden and extend our notion of the political beyond its historical sequestering from social reproduction and the private sphere. Thus, as we can never be emancipated, only less or more free ("governed like this, not like that," in Foucault's oft-cited phrase), we can never *be* a democracy, only less or more democratic.[15] Aspiration, collective identity, and practices, not settled form.[16]

Still, the dream of democracy persists: ruling ourselves in common so that we are not ruled by one or a few, by a part, by wealth, by technocracy, or by a liberalism that permits ferocious social and economic powers to reign. This dream promises shared participation in setting the terms of our existence, terms that do not sacrifice the many to the few on a hierarchical calculus or the few to the many on a utilitarian one. The dream is not premised on the ontological autonomy of politi-

168

cal life from other realms but on the uniqueness and nonfungibility of political power-sharing, its distinction from religious, moral, or familial realms of rule, and from the rule of the individual over itself in an appropriately protected personal sphere. Certainly the semiotics and contents of the political are inconstant across time and venue. Certainly the political is protean and contestable. It is a mistake to deify or reify it or to distinguish it sharply from the powers of production, reproduction, racialization, and everything else that its Aristotelian, Arendtian, and Schmittian variants fought to repel from its meaning and purview. In this regard, recognizing what has been historically excluded from the purview of the political, even by leftists, is vital to deepening and extending the project of democracy. (Social movements, such as Ni Una Menos and Black Lives Matter, do precisely this deepening and extending when they bring neglected injustices and violations into political discourse.) If, as Oksala suggests, I have underplayed these features of the political in some of my sentences, aiming to resurface its importance as the a priori of democratic rule, I accept the correction without revising the impulse. We cannot give up the object of the political— not the concept but the object, however indeterminate, changeable, and contestable it may be—without giving up on democracy itself.[17] Again, the political does not reference a particular thing or relation but the struggle over what is common and over the powers comprising and organizing that commonness. This is why the political cannot be equated with politicization; as Robin Celikates reminds us, the latter often reiterates and reflects conditions of de-democratization and even privatizing the common. Indeed, the contemporary politicization of journalism, courts, and education, far from rehabilitating political life as the domain of common concern, reduces it to interest and power grabs. The painful contemporary politicization of everyday life associated with political polarization—practices of consumption and style, pastimes, recreation, and family form—is a symptom of nihilistic devaluation or trivialization of value, not struggle over the significant powers organizing our common world.

All of this bears repeating because, despite endless homilies to "democracy" in the face of neofascist or authoritarian challenges today, the value of shared rule is not widely embraced in this age. It

169

is downplayed if not forthrightly rejected by neoliberals, technocrats, libertarians, and Leninists on the left and right, as well as anarchists. Still, reestablishing the value of shared rule barely begins the political theoretical conversation about democracy we require today. What is the terrain and terroir of democracy after the nation-state? Who is the "we" that would rule itself? How can democracy manage global powers, global dangers, and local democratic practices?

The first problem confronting democracy today is domain. Democracy is incoherent on a global scale. Its European postnational experiment has not gone well. Yet most on the left believe restricting democracy to nation-states can only be reactionary, hardening what Celikates, citing Nicholas de Genova, terms the "nationalist metaphysics of state power."[18] So, what about the subnational, the city, the neighborhood, the institution, the workplace? Étienne Balibar calls for workshops or laboratories of democracy.[19] Eric Olin Wright looks to non-state-centric practices of democracy in workplaces or in city budgeting, practices he hopes may be linked to each other and also be scaled up.[20] Sheldon Wolin approaches nonstatist democracy differently, identifying citizen initiatives and mobilizations as expressions of democracy's necessarily fugitive and episodic character, and treating institutions and constitutions as democracy's neutralization. Perhaps, especially but not only during the interregnum, localism and "occasionalism" remain the best ways of incubating and practicing democracy. Perhaps Tocqueville was right about municipal democracy as the necessary soil for building democratic culture in an era of large and centralizing power, the place where we learn together how to handle power and think beyond our own interests. Or perhaps Rousseau was correct that only in small republics could power be shared and a notion of "the common" be sustained. Certainly all of these approaches to democracy distinguish it from populism today, which rebels against distant elites, institutions, and transnational powers but does not advance a regime in place of the one that it protests against.[21] Of course, localism comes with many risks and limitations, from provincialism to limited capacity to challenge the global powers that set its conditions. This is also the case for most nations, of course, and returns us to the problem with which we began:

If global democracy is incoherent and the nation-state is exhausted, where is democracy to live?

The second, related problem confronting democracy today is democratic exclusion and popular sovereignty. For a people to rule themselves, they must be defined and circumscribed as a people. And democracy cannot dispense with sovereignty without being terribly attenuated in power and significance (exactly the attenuation the neoliberals aimed at in their attempt to discredit and dismember popular sovereignty). Democracy requires a constitutive "we," and hence an outside, a "not-us," as well as a right to self-determination. This "not-us" does not have to be a "they" and certainly need not comport with a Schmittian figure of enmity. To the contrary, solidarity and mutual aid among sovereign peoples is fully possible. Moreover, popular sovereignty can be layered or federated, direct or representative, cooperative or agonistic and contentious. It is possible for it to give itself limits, as rights do internally and transnational accords and regulations do externally. Still, for us to rule ourselves we must circumscribe ourselves. To be more than gestural and not reduced to the franchise, democracy must be a sovereign mode of exercising power.

We know and affirm this about democratic control of our cities, workplaces, or even universities. Those who live in them, not the international titans of finance and tech, ought to determine the shape and fate of urban neighborhoods. Those who are part of any democratized enterprise, not outsiders, should decide its practices and goals. Neither a faculty senate nor a trade union permits outsiders to vote on its proposals and memoranda. All of these are reminders that, for self-rule, we have to specify the boundaries of the self and secure our self-determination against external violation. Self-determination moved to the collective level does not do away with this; again, violation of popular sovereignty was at the heart of left outrage over the EU treatment of Greece in the aftermath of the financial crisis. Concern with this violation is also at the heart of protest against the destruction of local "food sovereignty" by agribusiness. It animates support for Indigenous sovereignty against the incursion of nation-states. Of course, a democratic people can welcome new members, care for and about nonmembers, and develop relations of solidarity with outsiders. It can affirm a "we" beyond its own. The requisite boundedness and sovereignty of democracy, with a clear demarcation of belonging, does not equate to policed territory or inhospitality or ruthlessness toward the nonbelonging, nor does it mitigate against open borders or world-regarding ecological and humanitarian commitments. It does, however, require settling who participates in and who is subject to its determinations.

The third problem confronting democracy today pertains to the global character of major powers and of existential threats. The former refers to dispersed capitalist production and supply chains, of course, but also to ethereal webs of finance, technology, and surveillance and even to networks of terror. The latter includes climate change above all but also species destruction, overfishing, and rainforest destruction; reduced biodiversity; and toxic production and waste, all of which would be devastating even if they were not raising the temperature of the planet. It is difficult to mobilize democracy to transform these powers and redress these problems. This is due in part to their global reach and unevenly experienced impact in a world still organized by nation-states and nationalistic policies, but also to the emergency nature of the climate crisis and the challenge of meeting it within a capitalist order or rapidly developing a successor to capitalism that is oriented entirely by long-term sustainability. And it is due to the nature of democracies themselves, in which, as the great republican theorists (Machiavelli, Rousseau, Tocqueville) warned us, privations are hard for a people to give to themselves.[22] This is as true for the historically privileged and entitled as for the historically disadvantaged and deprived. These reasons taken together explain why Joel Wainwright and Geoff Mann believe "Climate Leviathan" may be the best we can hope for.[23] They anticipate a planetary sovereign on the model of Hobbes's Leviathan for regulating extraction, production, and consumption. This sovereign, they suggest, might acquire popular legitimacy by protecting us from ourselves, but it features not a whisper of democratic self-rule.

If Wainright and Mann are right, we may have to approach global powers today in divided fashion: on the one hand, accepting a consolidated, undemocratic, but accountable global form of governance to contain and regulate these powers in order to prevent the apocalypse and extremes of exploitation, surveillance, and pillage; on the other hand, seeking to defang, or better, dismantle their capacity to generate that apocalypse and divest human beings of democratic control of their lives and of local, sustainable ways of life. Responsible left political theory cannot neglect either of these, but we have little experience with theorizing in these ways, which cannot be reduced to federalism, "layered sovereignty," or slogans about thinking globally and acting locally. We also have no idea whether it's possible to integrate these projects, especially on a worldwide scale. We are talking about something like inverted ordoliberalism: we need a global constitution establishing inviolable limits and enforced by fierce political agency, combined with diverse and empowered democratic forces everywhere. From below, democracy disseminated and attempting to handle a range of powers; from above, rules enforced without exception for securing the planet and its life forms from abuse and peril.

This, of course, is not the dream of any on the right, which brings us to the final problem that I want to mention: civil war. What are we going to do with our right-wing nationalists, both in and out of state power? Not only what are we going to do with their raging racism and ethnonationalism, so chillingly set out by Eduardo Mendieta in his opening, or their misogyny and patriarchalism, which exceed what Robyn Marasco and Johanna Oksala describe as the problem of neoliberal familialism. Or their dark twist on Bloch's "not all people exist in the same Now" that Loren Goldman examines and affirms exclusively for its left potentials. Or their strategic exploitation by plutocrats and megachurches. Rather, what are we going to do with them in view of the planetary emergency and the necessity of building a sustainable and just global future? What are we going to do with their hatred of democracy and equality, their privatization of freedom, in what remains of liberal democracy and in whatever we aspire to build as democracy's next iteration?

What are we going to do with them in Argentina and Brazil, Turkey and Egypt, India and Europe, Canada and Australia, the United States and Israel? Convert them? With what bait and promise? Right-wing platforms often offer their constituents more in the short run than we do. Wait for them to die off? There's no time for that, and in any case, they continue to recruit from the ranks of rancorous young white men in the Global North and from the dispossessed inhabiting the shanty-towns of the Global South. Overwhelm them demographically? Look at how that is going for Arab Israelis. Actual civil war? Which side has the guns and ammo?

What we can be sure of is that in a nihilistic age, appeals to interest, reason, facticity, futurity, and truth are largely beside the point, as is counting on transformations at the site of contradiction or irrationality. Fear, precariousness, lost boundaries and futures, and above all the fracturing of (white male) supremacy condition the rise of a nationalist Right, but attachment to illusion and indifference to truth spur it as well. This attachment and indifference return us to the nihilism with which we began. Combined with what Nietzsche called "the desire to will nothingness rather than not will," these things are iconic of nihilism, not working through it. Asynchronicity indeed.

This manifest indifference to truth, rather than attachment, also brings us to an important question in Eduardo Mendieta's chapter—namely, whether there is anything in genealogical politics and its rejection of progressivism that inherently links it with a left project. "On what grounds are we to challenge a particular presentation of the historical ontology of ourselves that may lead to an efficacious history? If the aim is to mobilize the present in a certain direction, . . . on what grounds can we persuade others to push in [the] direction [we want], once we have persuaded them of the artificiality of what we take to be immutable and the truth of history?"[24] Ay, there's the rub. Nothing in the struggle to reconceive history, and hence the present, guarantees a left truth at the level of critique of the present or vision for the future. Establishing that truth is an ongoing campaign, not an epistemological entailment of genealogy. This is not a concession to relativism but rather acknowledges the specificity of the political domain, where values rather than scientific truths, together with the histories that carry or dispossess these values, war with each other.[25] If this is dispiriting to the Left, it is a sign we are not yet over the idea that we alone have the truth about how the world ought to be organized, an idea that hews to the crudest progressivism.

Mendieta's chapter contains another query that may be helpful here. He rightly wonders whether Foucault really neglected the domain of the political, as I suggest, or whether the very idea of a political imaginary varying from neoliberal reason is wholly at odds with Foucault's for- mulation of governing reason or governmentality.[26] This hypothesized incompatibility, however, would arise from the very totalization Foucault sought to avoid, even as he identified governmentality with dissemination across everyday life, and a conduct of conduct, that vastly exceeds the powers associated with ideology. This is the fine edge we must walk to follow Foucault here, a walk he himself did not always manage. On the one hand, governmentality reaches deeper and disseminates further than beliefs and ideas to order, constitute, and govern us. On the other hand, governmentality and even governing rationalities are not totalizing; nothing on Foucauldian landscapes of genealogical tributaries and divergences, and of power's multiplicity, ever is.

How is it possible, otherwise, that both right and left political visions can take shape that do not comport with this order, that are only partly immanent to it and do not mirror it directly? How is it that right-wing activists can idealize a white Christian masculinist nationalism in retreat for decades and transmogrify it by tethering it to a class of the dispossessed? How is it that the Left can limn a commons in which we are neither unified and homogenized nor atomized and disintegrated, neither *omnes* nor *singulatum*, but sharing across difference at local and global levels? How does each envision futures that move well beyond neoliberal reason and even liberal political rationality? The political imaginary may turn out to be useful here in identifying a practice that contests the otherwise unbroken field of political reason.[27] With an accent on both terms—"political" understood as powers that arrange and affect us in common, however differently, and "imaginary" understood as lifting off from the givenness and empirics of the present—political imaginaries are partly interpretations of the existing order, partly maps that exceed them. They become vital in challenging what Asad Haider formulates as the essence of depoliticization: "the exclusion of values and practices that may be the site of social struggles."[28] If they carry utopias, in setting out from this place and time but not being fully bound by it, they function as granular critiques of the present, not escapes from it. (This is how Thomas More, one of utopia's early and most creative theorists, conceived its power.) Put differently, political imaginaries arise from a present whose normative grip is loosened by genealogy, thus preventing that grip from choking the future.

Of course we need more than Foucault here. We are in the orbit of novel psychic disinhibition, desperation, delusion, illusion, and all the terror, anxiety, and dread attending the politics of emergency. Reckoning with these requires culturally and historically infused accounts of the psychic formations in this conjuncture, accounts that shed the universalist and essentialist features of unreconstructed Freudianism. It means building on the first-generation Frankfurt School's recognition that psyches are formed not only by nuclear families but by historically specific forms of political economy (which themselves give particular shape to families). It means moving beyond the Frankfurt School to appreciate iterations of capitalism as entailing not only relations of production but specific modes of governing reason that bear on the psyche. It means moving beyond capitalism and neoliberalism to incorporate critical race, postcolonial, feminist, and queer theoretical accounts of the forces shaping psychic lives. As Asad Haider reminds us, only through appreciating such powers, and moving away from "instinct theory," will we generate adequate accounts of desublimated political energies and affect. Only then are we also positioned to comprehend the attractiveness of scapegoating, conspiracies, and other postsecular diabolical agents. In short, to escape the limitations of political and social behaviorism or neuropsychology in understanding ourselves today, we need a rich psychoanalysis of the predilections and vulnerabilities, attachments and illusions, in contemporary subjects. This richness involves deep historicity, a profound reading of social and cultural powers, and a reckoning with nihilism, each of which psychoanalysis reaches for and still mostly misses.

For political theory aiming to build possible alternatives to current conditions and trajectories, the order is a tall one. We must develop new venues and practices of democracy, distinguishing solidarity from popular sovereignty and resistance from regime, but meeting global forms of power with aspirational self-determination at the local or regional

level. We must incorporate these novel experiments with democracy into visions of just and sustainable futures built from political imaginaries of the present. We must generate a just, democratic, and sustainable successor to capitalism. And we must wrestle with the social and psy-   177
chic configurations and damages of the current conjuncture, the plastic human material on which building a better future depends. If we accept the difficulty, complexity, and necessity of meeting these challenges, both in our scholarship and in the world, there is a slight chance of our winning the civil war and having a planetary future in which that win would mean something.

NOTES

1. See Sheldon S. Wolin, "Political Theory as a Vocation," in *Fugitive Democracy and Other Essays*, ed. Nicholas Xenos (Princeton: Princeton University Press, 2016), 24–26.
2. I argued for the importance of interdisciplinarity to the future of political theory in Wendy Brown, "At the Edge," *Political Theory* 30, no. 4 (2002): 556–76.
3. It is Nietzsche who suggests that "the aspect of the earth is essentially altered" by fundamental historical shifts in humans themselves: "The existence on earth of an animal soul turned against itself, taking sides against itself, was something so new, profound, unheard of, enigmatic, contradictory, and pregnant with a future that the aspect of the earth was essentially altered." Friedrich Nietzsche, *On The Genealogy of Morals*, trans. and ed. Walter Kaufmann (New York: Random House, 1989), 85.
4. See the preface to Nietzsche's *Genealogy of Morals*; and Michel Foucault, "Nietzsche, Genealogy, History," in *The Foucault Reader*, ed. Paul Rabinow (London: Penguin, 1984), 95–97.
5. Denise Riley *"Am I That Name?": Feminism and the Category of "Women" in History* (Minneapolis: University of Minnesota Press), 6. She also writes, "Feminism has intermittently been as vexed with the urgency of disengaging from the category 'women' as it has with laying claim to it . . . constitutionally torn between fighting against over-feminisation and against under-feminisation, especially where social policies have been at stake" (3–4).
6. https://www.theguardian.com/us-news/video/2019/feb/23/dianne-feinstein-rebuffs-young-climate-activists-calls-for-green-new-deal-video.
7. In this regard, Hillary Clinton's 2016 campaign mantra, "Finishing What We Started" (from the earlier Clinton and Obama years), could not have been more tone deaf to this politics of emergency.
8. Dipesh Chakrabarty, "The Climate of History: Four Theses," *Critical Inquiry* 35, no. 2 (Winter 2009): 197–222

9. https://www.versobooks.com/blogs/3518-democracy-oppression-and-univer
sality-an-interview-with-etienne-balibar.

10. Wolfgang Streeck, "Europa braucht die Nation"; and https://wolfgangstreeck
.files.wordpress.com/2020/01/the-international-state-system-after-neoliberal
ism-journal-version.pdf.

11. Giorgio Agamben, Alain Badiou, Daniel Bensaïd, Wendy Brown, Jean-Luc
Nancy, Jacques Rancière, Kristin Ross, and Slavoj Žižek, *Democracy in What
State?* (New York: Columbia University Press, 2011), is one of many texts pos-
ing and exploring this question.

12. Oksala, in this volume.

13. "Regime," from the Latin *regere*, meaning "to direct or guide," and from *regi-
men*, meaning "guidance, direction, government, rule."

14. Oksala, in this volume.

15. Michel Foucault, "What Is Critique?," in *The Politics of Truth*, ed. Sylvère
Lotringer and Lysa Hochroth (New York: Semiotexte, 1997).

16. Sheldon Wolin took this further, insisting that institutionalization, including
constitutionalization, always stills democratic energies and demands. "Stated
somewhat starkly: constitution signifies the suppression of revolution; revolution, the destruction of constitution," he writes in "Norm and Form." Elsewhere
he adds, "Constitutionalism, especially in its Madisonian version, is designed to
strew as many barriers as possible to demotic power." Wolin, *Fugitive Democracy*, 77, 110.

17. Wolin puts this point the other way around: "Individuals who concert their
powers for low-income housing, worker ownership of factories, better schools,
better health care, safer water, controls over toxic waste disposals and a thou-
sand other common concerns of ordinary lives are experiencing a democratic
moment and contributing to the discovery, care and tending of a commonal-
ity of shared concerns. Without necessarily intending it, they are renewing the
political by contesting the forms of unequal power which democratic liberty
and equality have made possible." Ibid., 98–99.

18. Robin Celikates, in this volume.

19. See Étienne Balibar, *We the People of Europe? Reflections on Transnational Citizenship*, trans. James Swenson (Princeton: Princeton University Press, 2003),
28; and the 2020 interview for the Verso blog cited in note 9 above.

20. Eric Olin Wright, *How to Be an Anti-capitalist in the 21st Century* (London:
Verso, 2019), chaps. 5 and 6.

21. For a counter to this, see Biglieri and Cadahia, *Seven Essays on Populism*, trans.
G. Cicciarello-Maher (Cambridge, UK: Polity Press, 2021).

22. See Wendy Brown, "Why Is Democracy So Hard?," *Politics and Society*, Novem-
ber 2020, https://doi.org/10.1177/0032329220962655.

23. Joel Wainwright and Geoffrey Mann, *Climate Leviathan: A Political Theory of
Our Planetary Future* (London: Verso, 2020). They sketch other possibilities,
both darker and more emancipatory ones, but aim to be realistic in reckoning
with the likelihood of this one.

24. Mendieta, in this volume.

25. I developed this argument at length in the 2019 Yale Tanner Lectures on Human
Values, https://whc.yale.edu/past-tanner-lectures-human-values#lectures-block
_5-0.

26. Mendieta, in this volume.
27. Yves Winter has offered stern caution about the term "political imaginary," finding it vague, promiscuous, and deprived of the analytics of power carried by terms such as "ideology" and "governing." Other thinkers, from Cornelius Castoriadis to Martin Saar, have found it fecund. An entire issue of *Political Epistemology* was dedicated to this debate, https://www.tandfonline.com/doi/full /10.1080/02691728.2019.1652859, but I wonder if we ought to pause it in order to figure out what some are seeking to capture with the term that is unavailable in the existing lexicon of political theory.
28. Haider, in this volume.

CONTRIBUTORS

AMY ALLEN is Distinguished Professor of Philosophy and Women's, Gender, and Sexuality Studies at Penn State University. Her recent books include *The End of Progress: Decolonizing the Normative Foundations of Critical Theory* (Columbia University Press, 2016), *Critical Theory Between Klein and Lacan: A Dialogue*, coauthored with Mari Ruti (Bloomsbury Press, 2019), and *Critique on the Couch: Why Critical Theory Needs Psychoanalysis* (Columbia University Press, 2021). She has also coedited, with Eduardo Mendieta, *From Alienation to Forms of Life: The Critical Theory of Rahel Jaeggi* (Penn State University Press, 2018), the *Cambridge Habermas Lexicon* (Cambridge University Press, 2019), *Justification and Emancipation: The Critical Theory of Rainer Forst* (Penn State University Press, 2019), and *Decolonizing Ethics: The Critical Theory of Enrique Dussel* (Penn State University Press, 2021).

WENDY BROWN is UPS Foundation Professor in the School of Social Science at the Institute for Advanced Study. She is the author of *States of Injury: Power and Freedom in Late Modernity* (Princeton University Press, 1995), *Politics Out of History* (Princeton University Press, 2001), *Edgework: Critical Essays on Knowledge and Politics* (Princeton University Press, 2005), *Regulating Aversion: Tolerance in the Age of Identity and Empire* (Princeton University Press, 2006), *Walled States, Waning Sovereignty* (Zone Books, 2010), *Undoing the Demos: Neoliberalism's Stealth Revolution* (Zone Books, 2015), and most recently, *In the Ruins of Neoliberalism: The Rise of Antidemocratic Politics in the West* (Columbia University Press, 2019). In 2019, she delivered the Tanner Lectures on Human Values: "Power and Knowledge in Nihilistic Times: Thinking with Max Weber."

ROBIN CELIKATES is professor of social philosophy at the Freie Universität Berlin, codirector of the Humanities and Social Change Center Berlin, and a member of the *Critical Times* editorial team. Among his publications are the book *Critique as Social Practice: Critical Theory and Social Self-Understanding* (Rowman & Littlefield International,

2018) and numerous articles on disobedience, migration, and critical theory. For more on his work, visit https://fu-berlin.academia.edu /RobinCelikates.

LOREN GOLDMAN is assistant professor of political science at the University of Pennsylvania. He specializes in German and American thought and is currently completing a book on political hope. His work has appeared in *Political Theory*, *Theory & Event*, *Analyse & Kritik*, *Transactions of the Charles S. Peirce Society*, and *Journal of the Philosophy of History*, among other academic journals and edited volumes, and he co-translated Ernst Bloch's *Avicenna and the Aristotelian Left* (Columbia University Press, 2019). He studied at Yale University, the Goethe Universität Frankfurt, and the Universities of Oxford and Chicago, and has held postdoctoral fellowships at UC Berkeley and Rutgers.

ASAD HAIDER is assistant professor of politics at York University, a founding editor of *Viewpoint Magazine*, and the author of *Mistaken Identity* (Verso, 2018). His writings can be found in the publications *History of the Present*, *Radical Philosophy*, *Comparative Literature and Culture*, *The Baffler*, *n+1*, *The Point*, *Salon*, and elsewhere.

ROBYN MARASCO is professor of political science at Hunter College and The Graduate Center, CUNY. Her research has focused on developing the insights of critical theory, feminism, and psychoanalysis for political theory and interpretive social science. Her first book, *The Highway of Despair: Critical Theory After Hegel* (Columbia University Press, 2015), reconstructs the emancipatory project of critical theory around the idea of negative dialectics. Professor Marasco was guest editor of a special issue of *South Atlantic Quarterly* on "The Authoritarian Personality" and guest coeditor, with Banu Bargu, of a special issue of *Rethinking Marxism* on "The Political Encounter with Louis Althusser." She is also coeditor of *Polity*, a journal of political science.

EDUARDO MENDIETA is professor of philosophy and Latina/o studies, as well as affiliated faculty at the School of International Affairs and the Bioethics Program at Penn State University. He is the author of *The Adventures of Transcendental Philosophy* (Rowman & Littlefield, 2002) and *Global Fragments: Globalizations, Latinamericanisms, and*

Critical Theory (SUNY Press, 2007). He is also coeditor with Jonathan
VanAntwerpen of *The Power of Religion in the Public Sphere* (Columbia
University Press, 2011), with Craig Calhoun and Jonathan VanAntwer-
pen of *Habermas and Religion* (Polity, 2013), and with Stuart Elden of   183
Reading Kant's Geography (SUNY Press, 2011). Most recently, he coed-
ited, with Amy Allen, *From Alienation to Forms of Life: The Critical The-
ory of Rahel Jaeggi* (Penn State University Press, 2018), the *Cambridge
Habermas Lexicon* (Cambridge University Press, 2019), *Justification and
Emancipation: The Critical Theory of Rainer Forst* (Penn State Univer-
sity Press, 2019), and *Decolonizing Ethics: The Critical Theory of Enrique
Dussel* (Penn State University Press, 2021). He is the 2017 recipient of the
Frantz Fanon Outstanding Achievement Award.

JOHANNA OKSALA is the Arthur J. Schmitt Professor of Philosophy in
the Department of Philosophy at Loyola University Chicago. Her areas
of expertise are political philosophy, feminist philosophy, environmental philosophy, Foucault, and phenomenology. Oksala is the author of
five monographs and over fifty refereed journal articles and book chapters in her areas of expertise. Her work has been translated into eight
languages. Her books include *Foucault on Freedom* (Cambridge University Press, 2005), *Foucault, Politics, and Violence* (Northwestern University Press, 2012), and *Feminist Experiences* (Northwestern University
Press, 2016).

INDEX

Page numbers with an *n* refer to a footnote or an endnote.

193

Milton Keynes UK
Ingram Content Group UK Ltd.
UKHW011835021023
429801UK00005B/430